Praise for
Podcast Guest Profits

“Technology continues to open new doors of opportunity with massive knowledge and information. But creating a business requires more than knowledge. Fortunately, now we have a manual from an engineer to harness, apply and profit from the wonderful emerging opportunity in podcasting.”

Dan Miller
Creative Thinker, Podcaster. and *New York Times* Best Selling Author of *48 Days to the Work You Love*

“Tom’s prescriptions for your podcasting future are bold and original. Electrifying insights crackle off every page of this volume filling you with inspirational visions of the destination along with the specific practicalities for reaching it. Grab this book and get to work.”

Rabbi Daniel Lapin
Podcast host and *New York Times* Best Selling Author of *Thou Shall Prosper*

"Tom has mastered the art of delivering free and valuable content on the amazing medium of podcasting. Now, he's shared the system he has perfected so that you can model to grow your authority, business, and revenue!"

John Lee Dumas
Podcast host of EOFire.com

"*Podcast Guest Profits* has the rare combination of great vision and tactical execution. Not only does this book paint a new vision for a supposedly "old" digital medium, but Tom's specific suggestions around growth and optimization make it a must-read."

Sam Mallikarjunan
Principal Marketing Strategist for HubSpot
Co-Author of *How to Sell Better than Amazon*

"*Podcast Guest Profits* is the book I can recommend to the entrepreneur, coach, author, etc., who wants to grow their business predictably, effectively, and profitably. Tom is a genius in both knowledge and application. Fortunately, he's also a genius when it comes to teaching others how to do the same."

Bob Burg
New York Times Best Selling co-author of *The Go-Giver*

"*Podcast Guest Profits* is THE quintessential book to help you learn how to turn your podcast interviews into real dollars. But, perhaps, more importantly it provides a clear, concise and easy to follow roadmap on how to communicate with an audience and connect with your ideal customers. If you are trying to grow your business, increase your impact and better connect with your ideal customers, *Podcast Guest Profits* is a must-read!"

Josh Brown, Esq.
Franchise lawyer and host of the *Franchise Euphoria Podcast*

"Podcasts offer the unique ability to share your message with your exact target audience using your own personal voice. Your voice is powerful in the process of people coming to know, like and trust you. Tom is an expert at helping people share their message in front of the right audiences through podcast interviews. Not only that, he also has amazing insights on how to you can make the most out of every podcast guest opportunity."

Cliff Ravenscraft
The Podcast Answer Man

"Tom's story is compelling, but what truly gets me fired up about this book, is the expertise Tom has in helping you get your message out to the world through the amazing channel of podcasting. I love the 30-day action plan. Each step along the way is designed to expose your brand, amplify your message and with surgical precision and cut through the noise created in this crowded marketplace. Take a shortcut to success and to profit, do yourself a huge favor and read Tom Schwab's *Podcast Guest Profits.* You'll be glad you did."

Doug Sandler
Author, speaker, and co-host of the *Nice Guys on Business Podcast*

PODCAST GUEST PROFITS

GROW YOUR BUSINESS

WITH A TARGETED INTERVIEW STRATEGY

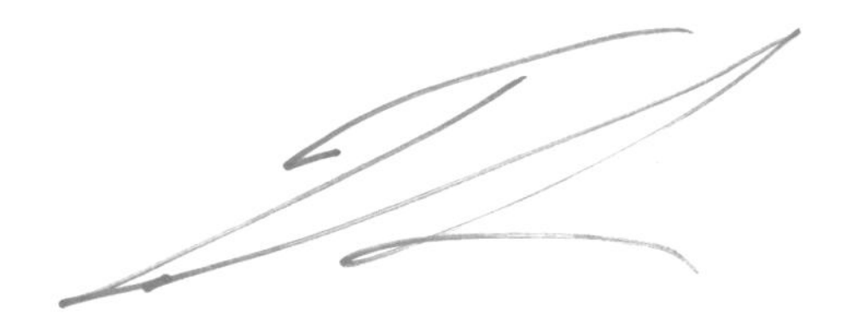

Tom M. Schwab

PODCAST GUEST PROFITS

Published by Interview Valet

ISBN 978-0-9982806-0-8

Printed in the United States of America
2016

CONTENTS

ACKNOWLEDGMENTS

To put my name on this work seems to be somewhat disingenuous.

Everything you read exists because someone first taught me. All of my teachers, mentors, and those who asked me "why?" caused me to think deeper. They all deserve the credit. While the entire list is longer than the book there are a few I want to mention.

The Nuclear Navy who taught me results come from teachable reproducible systems.

My customers: You are the true experts You told me what you loved and what you loathed. You saw my vision, your possibilities and had the faith in me to test this crazy strategy. Together we learned, refined, and continue to improve this system.

My Mastermind: Your friends want you to be happy. Your mastermind want you to be better. At every point you gave me the encouragement, resources, ideas and feedback. You made the mere idea of a book into a reality.

My family: Before it was written down, this book was talked out over and over again. My family listened, asked questions, and sometimes just politely faked interest.

My wife: In chemistry sometimes all the elements can be present, but the reaction doesn't happen without the catalyst. Karen is my catalyst. Through her love, encouragement, prayers and insight my life has produced more in 14 year with her than the 37 year without her.

My God: Often I feel like the child who proudly proclaims "look what I did" when everyone else knows it was his father behind him that did 99% of the work. The nuns and monks who taught me in school can attest: All the glory goes to Him.

You, my readers: Success is what you do for yourself. Significance is what you do for other. I pray you will make this book significant by taking the ideas and executing on them. You have something to share that will help your ideal customers. Talk directly to them. Serve them. Grow your business as a podcast guest.

FOREWORD

I spent four decades as a small business owner and have never been as excited about the future of business than I am today.

As I reflect back over my past successes, I'm reminded of many challenges and obstacles I and other small business owners faced. Marketing ranks at or very near the top of the list of challenges for me and many freelancers, entrepreneurs, or business owners I have met over the decades. Marketing was something I was not very good at early in my career, and I wasn't alone.

Gone are the days where you only need to have a quality product or service in order to make a good living because media and internet marketing has eliminated boundaries and made it just as easy—and sometimes easier— to buy something from around the world as it is to by it from around the corner.

The quality of your product or service is still critically important for your long-term success, but if nobody knows you exist, it won't matter much because your business will be short lived. In fact, having a superior product and world -class service is paramount, but it's often overlooked in a congested marketplace.

When I shifted from brick and mortar to an online business at the beginning of 2014, I knew I was facing a significant challenge. My business, *View from the Top,* was a premier life and business coaching service that could help men live a life of success and significance in business and at home, but what good was that if nobody knew I existed?

Forty years of brick and mortar business seemed easy compared to the vast and seemingly endless marketing tactics we're inundated with online. From social media, to search engine optimization, to pay-per-click advertising, to teleseminars, webinars, and more, it's nearly impossible to know where to start. For the first time, I needed a strategy that allowed me to identify and connect with my ideal customers because hanging a sign and putting an ad in the local paper was not enough.

Beyond the tactics, I had never been required to speak to the masses, nationally or internationally. My focus always had been the surrounding counties, not countries, and my audience was familiar with me and my businesses.

It was the first time in forty years of business that I felt lost, sitting at my desk with a world-class service, with decades of experience, knowledge, and wisdom, but no idea how to market it effectively to my ideal customers

A few weeks later, in what you might call a coincidence, but what I call divine intervention, I struck up a conversation at a chance mastermind meeting with a guy named Tom Schwab. Tom and I had never met, but our conversation was lively and I immediately felt comfortable with him. He was professional and mild-mannered with a pleasant sense of humor.

After several minutes I learned that Tom was an engineer and had even run nuclear reactors in the Navy, which was pretty impressive and intimidating because my last day of formal education was my last day of high school. Tom was clearly bright, articulate, and personable with his own decades of business experience that he managed to transition to an online presence.

When I asked Tom for advice about how to do the same for *View from the Top,* he shared several online marketing techniques with me. Each of them made so much sense. I was clearly in the presence of a master and did not want to pass up the opportunity in front of me.

By the end of the conversation, I asked Tom to help me clarify the best way to grow my online presence, connect with my ideal customers, and grow my business.

Over the next several weeks Tom and I worked closely to design a strategy that focused on becoming a guest on podcasts whose listeners were my ideal customers. Tom identified the shows, helped me design a simple web process for client nurturing, and set up a back end to help us analyze and measure everything about the process to continuously improve the effectiveness of the campaign.

The results were immediate. After my very first podcast interview I knew I had found my answer. Tom knew exactly what to do. All I needed to do was show up and talk with podcast hosts about my story, my four decades in business, and how men (my ideal customers) could learn from my experiences to live their best lives. At the end of the conversation, I'd share a way for men to get in touch with me and get even more substantive help to improve their lives.

At first dozens, then hundreds, and then thousands of people flooded to me within weeks and by the end of the year I had a full client roster and a wait list of people wanting to work with me. I then added additional services to allow the men on my waitlist to connect with me in other ways to help them just like I would help my one-on-one clients.

Tom and I analyzed and documented everything we did during that time and shared it with other business owners in other industries he was working with to design a strategy that is effective and convenient no matter what industry you're in or what product or service you sell.

Two years, and thousands of interviews later, Tom told me he was turning the process we used into an easy-to-use guide so other freelancers, entrepreneurs, and small business owners could replicate the process for their businesses and avoid the same feeling of being lost in the vast wilderness of the internet that I felt at the beginning of 2014.

Podcasts Guest Profits is that guide. The lessons in this book changed my life. They changed my family's life. And they've allowed me to help other men change their lives for the better by connecting with me and other men who are building lives of success and significance.

I am forever grateful that Tom was willing and able to show me the ropes at the very beginning of my coaching practice. Little did I know that I could speak to thousands, and now millions of potential clients about my newly-formed company from the convenience of my home office and that it could be so simple to do, even for a guy like me who had no college education and little comfort with technology.

The kind of exposure I got with the systems Tom outlines in this book would have cost me tens of thousands of dollars and hundreds of hours of my time, but all I needed with Tom's method was a good microphone, an internet connection, and thirty minutes of my time, and I was up and running on a highly-ranked podcast, *Entrepreneur On Fire,* talking with hundreds of thousands of listeners with John Lee Dumas.

To date, I have completed hundreds of interviews, and I have not scratched the surface of the endless possibilities.

It seems so surreal that this marketing tactic is so useful and yet so affordable. Tom has month after month and year after year perfected this method to an absolute science.

It has been an honor and delightful experience to work alongside such a man of honesty and integrity. If you follow Tom's suggestions in this book, I'm confident that your life and business will be equally impacted.

I would love to continue writing, but it's time for my next podcast interview.

Aaron Walker
President/Founder
View from the Top

ViewFromTheTop.com

INTRODUCTION

If you're frustrated watching others seemingly leap to success while you struggle to start or grow your business, you're not alone. You can't go ten minutes without hearing a "rags-to-riches in less than a year" story. At the same time, you work all day, take care of your household or family obligations all evening, and then trudge down to the basement for three or four more hours after everyone else is asleep to work on "growing your platform" to expand or start your business.

After months or years of late nights, early mornings, and lost weekends, what do you have to show for it? The doubts creep in. Are you good enough? Maybe people just don't connect with your message. Maybe the industry is just too crowded. You read every business book, try every new strategy or technique, work hard to expand your social media following, attend offline networking events, participate in dozens of Facebook groups, engage in Twitter chats and LinkedIn conversations. You're sliced so thin that it's almost impossible to keep up, and sometimes you don't. When you ask others for help or advice, many people will give you a two-minute answer, often with good intentions, but rarely with good advice. You're left even more confused.

I understand your frustrations. I've been there. I graduated from the U.S. Naval Academy in 1987 with a Bachelor's degree in Mechanical Engineering. My first job out of college was running a nuclear power plant. I know, looking back it does seem like quite a risk to hand the keys to a nuclear power plant to a guy fresh out of college, but the keys came with a manual. I followed the manual. After five years at the nuclear power plant, I moved on, working for twelve years in manufacturing, operations, and sales for a large medical device company. At every step there were manuals.

After seventeen years of working for other companies, I decided to start my first business. No matter how hard I looked, however, there was no manual. I'd never run a business without a manual. I wasn't even sure if it were possible to run a business over the long term without one, so I decided to create my own small business manual. Because I am an early adopter and marketer at heart and engineer by training, I spent the next decade or so identifying problems and designing systems to solve them. During that time, I went back to school to get my MBA with a concentration in marketing. I also learned and perfected inbound marketing outside of the formal education system, in my business. At the time, the term "inbound marketing" was new to the business world and was seen as a tool that used cutting-edge digital tools. While that was true, the foundational strategy was old. It was the same permission-based marketing method our great-grandparents used to get known, build trust, and turn visitors into raving life-long advocates. My business grew and eventually began operating efficiently without my constant attention.

As my business needed less and less of me, I began connecting with other business owners to assist them with growing their businesses. A theme emerged during my work with those business owners. No matter how well their businesses performed, they were all frustrated with two things. First, they lamented the lack of systems, feeling they needed to spend "too much time working in their business instead of on their business," as author Michael Gerber coined it. They wanted systems to follow to grow their business without them needing to do it all.

Second, they were frustrated by the difficulties in getting the attention of their ideal customers. They were frustrated and burned out. They had a terrific product, service, or message that could add tremendous value in the market, and some even change the world as we know it, but not enough people know who they were. Their biggest problem was that in a noisy world, they were totally obscure. Nobody they wanted to serve could hear them.

They had the same challenges that our parents, grandparents, and great-grandparents faced in business: a lack of systems and attention. The only issue was that while the challenges were the same, the tactics that worked for past generations didn't work anymore. I learned in the military that all tactics have an expiration date. A tactic that worked great in the past may not work today. The constant in any business was the mental and emotional process that a consumer goes through in taking notice and making a purchasing agreement. That didn't change. Consumers have always and still made buying decisions based on the same factors. People prefer to buy a product or service from someone they know, like, and trust. That is the unchanging strategy: Get ideal potential customers to know like and trust you. The tactics to efficiently and effectively reach those consumers, however, are constantly changing. New technologies emerge and the fight for attention always gets more crowded.

It was important to recognize that any worthwhile strategy to solve those two frustrations needed to incorporate the tactics of today (and tomorrow) with the time-tested consumer decision indicators. Over the next several months, I spent countless hours developing systems to help entrepreneurs and small business owners get noticed. To go from obscure to acclaimed. I was determined to crack the code of efficient and effective brand building. I tested, documented, adjusted, and tested again, working with small businesses and entrepreneurs to help them go from "who's that" to one of the "who's who" in their industry.

Back in the early 2000s the starting point would have been by building a website or blog. Websites or blogs used to be the best way for entrepreneurs and small business owners to showcase their products, services, and expertise in the digital world. Only a few years later a website and blog had become merely a requirement to be seen as legitimate, but they were no longer enough to stand out.

By that time, if you wanted to be noticed you needed to grow a presence on social media. New platforms exploded from Myspace, to Facebook, Twitter, LinkedIn, Instagram, Pinterest, Periscope, you name it. You were challenged with increasing followers, engagement, likes, shares, pins, re-pins, retweets, and more...everywhere.

Somewhere in the middle of that social media boom was the seemingly-way-too-niche medium of podcasts. As Myspace got sold for $500 million, and Facebook, Twitter, and LinkedIn cashed in with multi-billion-dollar public offerings, podcasts quietly grew, slowly but steadily, at least in relative terms.

At first, podcasts were mostly ignored by the mainstream, being perceived as relevant to only a small subset of a very technical group of people. Podcasters were viewed as amateurs, hobbyists, and podcasting got about as much attention and respect as ham radio. On top of that, marketing departments believed that the costs of producing and promoting a podcast were high, including equipment, learning curves, and time commitment required to plan, record, edit, and promote a podcast episode compared to a blog or social media content, which was at most a few dollars per month and required no new equipment.

That perception kept many people away from podcasts for years. Over time, however, the power of podcasts became unavoidable. Stories about entrepreneurs like John Lee Dumas of Entrepreneur On Fire, who turned a podcast into a multi-million-dollar businesses, hit the mainstream. Success stories about people who left corporate America to podcast became more frequent. Some, like Pat Flynn from the Smart Passive Income Podcast, started to publicly post monthly revenue reports from their shows. By that time, podcasts could no longer be ignored. Soon thereafter, mainstream media launched podcasts and podcast networks, as they realized that their perceptions about the cost-benefit of producing and promoting a show were wrong. Celebrities launched podcasts; and podcasts created celebrities. The power of the podcast was no longer a secret.

On top of that, as the movement towards podcasts became more pronounced, service providers emerged who you could pay to help alleviate some of the time-consuming tasks such as editing and promoting shows.

Tens of thousands of podcasts were born. Stay-at-home parents launched shows to help other parents raise their kids. Subject matter experts launched podcasts to show off their expertise. Business owners launched podcasts to talk directly to their customers. Gamers shared tips and tricks. Movie lovers shared reviews. You name it, there was—and is—a podcast about it.

As podcasting continued to develop, businesses and entrepreneurs realized that the power of the podcast is threefold.

First, it literally puts your voice in the head of the listeners. They get to know you. They drink their morning coffee, go for a run, or share a commute with you. They get to know, like, and trust you.

Second, a podcast is less prone to mental distractions than other mediums of content. Although a listener might be commuting, running, or emptying the dishwasher while listening to you, their earbuds literally block out many distractions that things like reading a book or website don't. Moreover, if they get thirsty or hungry while listening to you they don't need to turn their attention away from you. They simply stand up and take you with them to the fridge.

Finally, podcasts have less competition. While in 2016 there were hundreds of millions of websites and blogs, there were by comparison just over 300,000 podcasts in the United States. That is a lot of shows, for sure, but when you consider that this is broken down into hundreds or thousands of unique topics, a podcaster might be one of a few, a few hundred, or a few thousand podcasts on a topic compared to one in millions with a website or blog. On top of the lesser competition, access to podcasts has skyrocketed, no longer requiring an iPod or even a smart phone. Episodes can now be downloaded directly to the dashboard of a car. Listening to a podcast on a commute thus became the on-demand, often commercial-free option that consumers, and commuters craved.

All of those advantages make a compelling case for starting a podcast. But as you know by now, starting and running a podcast takes a lot of work. Work equals costs in terms of time, if done by you, or money, if done by someone else.

How much? It depends on the format, however even a quality one-host, no guest podcast that is thirty minutes long and released once per week will take the average weekend warrior at least two hours from start to finish divided between minimally preparing for the show, recording, editing, adding graphics and descriptions, and crafting blog-style "show notes" to promote your show. Anyone who says doing a podcast is easy or fast has either never done one or never done it well.

As a small business owner, engineer, and marketing consultant, I know that spending two hours per week for one thirty-minute show that only one audience will hear is a high price to pay. Increase the length or number of episodes, or add an interviewee with whom you will need to coordinate, prepare extra for by learning about them and their brands, and the cost increases even more, and you could easily spend five or more hours per week just getting your podcast episodes together and promoted.

There had to be a better way, I thought, to maximize the potential benefits of the podcast platform while minimizing the time or financial costs. I analyzed all of the potential costs and benefits of podcasting for business development and identified the most important goals for all people involved in podcast production and consumption, including audience members, podcast hosts, and podcast guests. At the end, I came up with a theory that I thought was the most practical and effective use of podcasts for everyone involved.

Feeling like I was starting to develop something pretty powerful, I reached out to a client of mine, Aaron Walker of View from the Top, to see whether he would be interested in helping me test my theory and design and refine my system. Aaron had been a business owner in Nashville, Tennessee, for over three decades. After selling his last business he decided he wanted to use the many lessons he learned in business and life to help other men live lives full of success and significance. I knew his products and services would be top notch and that the world needed his wisdom, so I thought he would be a perfect test candidate.

Aaron and I had first worked together using inbound marketing techniques to attract customers to Aaron and his website through content creation, mostly blog posts. Aaron and I wrote blog posts, put them up on his website, and promoted them through is existing channels. Like most other websites, one to two percent of the visitors turned into leads for Aaron's products and services. As with many inbound marketing campaigns, Aaron and I quickly grew frustrated because we knew that it would take at least a year to gain any traction.

Aaron is well spoken and confident. He has a great voice, with the southern twang of Zig Ziglar and the depth of James Earl Jones. That voice doesn't come across at all in blog posts. We knew that podcasts were a better option for him to establish deep connections with his target audience. I shared some of my analysis with Aaron and we considered whether he should start a podcast himself. Aaron is a smart business man and looking to get results quickly He also understood the importance of maximizing results while minimizing his investment of time and money. Based on these requirements we came to the opinion that starting a podcast did not seem like a wise option. Aaron did not have the time to invest or the will to learn how to podcast well and, just like a blog, did not want to start out from zero.

By that time I had the first iteration of my podcast-guest system in place, along with statistics to back up my theory that you could maximize the benefits of utilizing podcasts as a promotional tool while minimizing the investment of time required to do so through an organized campaign as a podcast guest. Although creating a podcast can be an effective way to develop a loyal audience, brand recognition, and authority over time, I theorized, small business owners can create much greater value for podcast listeners, podcast hosts, and themselves (and do so much faster), by developing an organized and deliberate campaign to build momentum as a podcast guest. An organized podcast guest campaign, I surmised, would reach more people because you would speak to the audiences of several shows and not just your own audience, while providing them content was relevant and meaningful to them. This focus on providing top-quality content within the context of each show to give maximum value to the podcast listeners would provide extraordinary value to podcasters and their listeners. It would also require a much smaller investment of time and money for the guest compared to launching a podcast.

"What if we could go to where your customers already are?" I asked Aaron. "What if we could get on podcasts that were already established and listened to by your ideal customer? You could be interviewed there. You could prepare in advance. Listeners would get to know, like, and trust you on the podcast. Then they would visit your site and connect further with you." I shared my analysis with Aaron. He was intrigued and immediately agreed to help test my system and develop best practices.

The initial plan for Aaron became to use the podcast interviews to direct quality leads to our already-established inbound marketing machine. We began reaching out to podcasts who we knew had a strong male audience of business owners, as this was his ideal client. After the first few interviews, we were so amazed by the results that we doubled down on our efforts. The webpage we directed listeners to on the interviews were the best performing I'd ever seen with inbound marketing. Conversion rates of visitors to leads went from one to two percent with blogs, to routinely converting at twenty-five to fifty percent with podcast interviews. When people heard Aaron, they quickly got to know him. Listening to him they got to like and trust him. Then they came to his website ready to take the next step. They arrived engaged and motivated to work with him.

Originally we wondered if this was because of Aaron's personality or market. As a good engineer, I test everything. I tried this strategy myself and reached out to several other small business owners to test. I wanted to understand the magic I had seen to see if it was a one-time miracle or a real marketing system. I attempted to eliminate as many variables as possible. We found businesses with different industries. We found guests with various voices. The only thing we avoided were people who had large existing audiences because we wanted to prove using a targeted podcast guest strategy could grow your business and take you from obscure to acclaimed across different industries.

The results were outstanding. The system worked. It began helping business owners find and connect with their ideal customers without leaving the comfort of their own home or office. Moreover, it helped people across industries, including industries as diverse as franchise sales, to life coaching, to quilting, to other physical and digital product sales. My clients were getting more noticed, collecting more leads, and securing more business in a matter of weeks with targeted podcast interviews than they had over the course of months or years with other strategies.

They found my system easier, too. It did not require them to commit to releasing fresh blog posts over and over. It did not require investing tens of thousands of dollars. It did not even require them to leave the comfort of your own home or office, to make a meaningful impact.

The power of the system is the system itself. Once it's set up, you control how fast and efficiently it runs. It can be scaled up or down as you grow your business. You can control the output and decide you want more or less business. It can be completely do-it-yourself or mostly outsourced, it's up to you.

The results were consistent. The system worked for everyone who implemented it. Podcast interviews drove engaged traffic, which led to more leads and customers. Soon thereafter the system began to take even more shape, from identifying the right podcasts, to how to engage with the podcast host, to how to set up an efficient and effective system to turn listens into leads and then leads into customers. It wasn't magic; it was a system.

The system was also simple. It was important to me that you didn't need to be an engineer, have an MBA, have run a nuclear power plant, or have already grown a business to run without you, to make any of it work. It was important to me that anyone looking to make quality connections with the right people in a short period of time could have a true do-it-yourself system. It was important to me that assistance from others to use the system would be purely for efficiency, and not out of necessity.

As the system was refined, results were also enhanced. In the first year working with Aaron, he was a guest on over one hundred podcasts, and spoke to well over two million ideal customers. From those interviews, Aaron followed the exact steps I will outline for you in this book. He filled up his schedule for one-on-one coaching, and then filled up his waiting list. As demand grew, he launched several group-coaching mastermind programs, which quickly filled up as well. Once demand grew larger than his capacity for one-on-one or even small group coaching, he launched a larger community, which now boasts well over two hundred members who each pay a monthly subscription fee to connect with Aaron for content, insights, and direction.

In just one year, Aaron went from an obscure, albeit excellent coach to creating demand that far exceeded his capacity, allowing him to scale his coaching practice. Aaron attributed all of that success to the exposure he gained to his ideal customers as a podcast guest.

The strategy also helped his social media following. Aaron also grew his Facebook fan page to over 3,000 likes, his Twitter following to over 2,000 followers, and his LinkedIn connections to over 3,000 connections.

Being a podcast guest helped him get found on Google and other search engines. With his true southern charm, Aaron says that "you couldn't find me with a bloodhound before I started doing podcast interviews." Now with all the back links from his appearance, Aaron is on the first page of Google for most all relevant keywords.

Like I mentioned, however, it wasn't just Aaron who experienced extraordinary results as a podcast guest. For example, franchisor Matt Miller, of School Spirit Vending, had spent six months trying to find people looking to invest tens of thousands of dollars for a franchise opportunity before working with me. During that time, Matt collected less than five leads. In the first thirty days of implementing the system I show you in this book, Matt collected almost fifty leads. In the first year of using this podcast guest strategy, Matt attributes over 50 new franchisees directly to podcast interviews.

In fact, even the most popular podcasters in the world recognize the value of being on other people's podcast.

Alex Harris of the Marketing Optimization Podcast, for example, has gone on record as saying that he doesn't get clients from his own podcast; he gets clients by going on other people's podcasts.

Cliff Ravenscraft, who is known as the Podcast Answer Man, spoke at the largest convention of podcasters about the power of being a guest and revealed that "the single greatest way I have found to grow my audience is to be a guest on other podcasts."

Even John Lee Dumas of Entrepreneur On Fire, a podcast with well over one million downloads each month, conducted a month-long podcast guest tour to promote his crowdfunding campaign to launch a goal-setting journal, a campaign that raised hundreds of thousands of dollars.

Finally, Chris Ducker of Virtual Staff Finder and the popular Virtual YOUPreneur Podcast, conducted the majority of his book launch through a podcast guest campaign.

The system I am about to share with you is the exact system that helped Aaron fill up his schedule and scale his business. It's the same system that Matt Miller used to go from five leads in six months to nearly fifty leads in thirty days. You will get all of the details of the system in this book, everything I developed over the course of more than two years and one thousand interviews. On top of that, I have set up a special page just for readers of this book to download free forms, checklists, and more at www.PodcastGuestProfits.com/Resources. In addition, all of the resources I talk about in this book are on that page, plus more, so be sure to bookmark it so you can get started building your business right away.

This isn't magic, it's a system. It's the manual I always wanted to grow my business. I found it, tested it, and perfected it. Now I share it with you, right here.

As podcasts continue to grow in popularity, more and more of your ideal customers are going to be listening to someone on a podcast. The only question is whether that will be you or your competitors. By using this system, you can make sure they aren't only listening to you, but connecting with you after the interview as well.

HOW TO READ THIS BOOK

Reading is an incredibly expensive exercise, not because of the cost of a book, but because of the time it takes to read. I realize you have given up your valuable time to read this, so with that, I want to make sure that you get the most value from it.

Regardless of what it says on my Naval Academy ring, knowledge isn't power, knowledge is the potential for power. As an engineer, I know that to get power you need fuel, a machine with a powerful engine, and a spark. This book will give you the information you need and a thirty-day plan to get started right away, but you need to provide the spark. Only you can take action.

With that in mind, here are the three types of people who will read this book, along with my best recommendation for how to read it to get the most value.

The first type of person is the do-it-yourself-er. If you want to replicate exactly what I have done myself and with my clients, you can do it by reading this book and going step-by-step through the process. Study the materials and answer the questions at the end of every chapter. You can also find additional resources, new information, checklists, worksheets, and more, on the resources page connected to this book at www.PodcastGuestProfits.com/Resources. You really can do this all yourself.

The second type of person is the person who wants to get the benefits out of the system, but who wants someone else to implement the system for them. For you, this will be an easier and faster read. If you read the table of contents, the introduction, the chapter on outsourcing, and the summary at the end you will have enough information to know what needs to be done. Then give this book to the person who will be implementing the strategy for you for them to read and take action.

The third type of person is the experienced executive who wants to understand the big picture only and delegate the rest. For you, you can get the value by reading the table of contents, the introduction, and the summary at the end. This way, you will familiarize yourself with the general steps and then hand off the book to the people or agency who will handle all of the details.

Either way, this proven strategy is an incredible way to connect better with more ideal customers. It's a marketing machine that you can fuel by conducting free podcast interviews. You will turn listeners into leads. You will go from being obscure to acclaimed faster than you ever believed was possible.

section one

CREATING THE FUEL

WHO DO YOU WANT TO SPEAK WITH?

My grandfather once told me "you can't choose who you work with." It's the only lie he ever told me. For him, it was reality, of course. He ran an auto-service station decades ago, so his customers were people who lived in his small town of St. Charles, Illinois, and if he got lucky, others who lived within a ten-mile radius of his station. He couldn't be choosy about who his customers would be. They drove in. He served them.

We have never before been able to go outside of our geographic boundaries like we can now. Because of that, for you and me, "you can't choose who you work with" is a lie. We now have direct access to billions of people right in our pockets. The entire world can be our marketplace through the free or low-cost technology and interconnection that we enjoy today. We can—and must—be choosy with whom we decide to work. We must chose to work with people who energize us and to whom we can provide the most value. This decision is fundamental to the start of any business. It's also fundamental to your effective marketing plan. No matter what tactics you use, marketing at its core is a discussion with someone who could be an ideal customer. Marketing is a conversation.

Using the right tactics, in the right way, will help you make sure that you're having the right discussions with the right people. I'm sorry to break the news to you, but most of those billions of people aren't your potential customers.

My agency worked with an author who came to us wanting to promote his book. When we talked about his ideal audience, he told us he wanted to talk to "everyone on podcasts." "If they have $20 for my book I want them to hear me on a podcast." We'll tell you what we told him. Some people on podcasts don't speak your language, some can't afford your product or services, and most don't need or want what you have to sell. Thus, the first step in my system is designed to help you find that small subset of people you can serve the best and who are both profitable to and potential advocates for your company.

Who do you want to speak with?

Many marketers guide you to identify one ideal customer, or avatar, for you to target through your marketing efforts. Synthesizing all the information at your fingertips into one ideal customer is a useful process to gain clarity into what type of products or services they may prefer or where you might find your future dream customers. It's important that you don't lose sight of the bigger picture when doing so, though. Many beginning marketers concentrate on the demographic side of defining their avatar. I think of demographics as things that the census bureau knows such as their age, marital status, education level, income, and zip code. While helpful, that says nothing about the psychological side of marketing, where buying decisions are made. That's why it's critical for you to discover the motivations of the people you want to reach and how you can connect to them through your story, products, and services. For this, it's necessary to dive deeper into the psychographics of your avatar.

The challenge with psychographics is that it includes information that most people don't readily share. It's the more important psychological elements, such as their motivations, fears, or aspirations. These insights aren't generally shared outside of their close friends or family members. On top of that, identifying what they already think about your industry, how they make buying decisions, who influences them, where they consume content, or where and how they prefer to connect, are all items that are difficult to gather.

Fortunately, difficult in this case doesn't mean time-consuming or costly. In fact, there are all kinds of ways to collect this information.

If you're already in business, you can gather psychographic data through sending a brief survey to your current customers. After all, the people who already pay for your products or services are one of the best sources of information for determining what would motivate more people just like them to connect with you. You could also brainstorm with people in your organization who know your customers the best, like salespeople or customer service representatives.

If you're new to business, you can learn from other business owners who have similar or complementary products. You can learn from others who already serve your ideal customers. You can also learn from small groups of friends or others in your network who are your ideal customer or understand your avatar. Just make sure they're willing to be completely honest about your presentation, prices, products, and services.

Please remember that the information doesn't need to be perfect, especially when starting out. The picture you put together can and should be continually refined based on customer feedback and ongoing operations. As time passes and your information gets better and better, your ideal buyer persona will become clearer. This allows you to become even more focused and more effective in your marketing.

Once you begin to develop your ideal buyer persona profile, break it down into no more than three to five segments based on factors relevant to your business. For example, if you have different products or services, or different versions or price points, you may find that the overall, general buyer persona for your business can be adjusted slightly to allow you to better target particular products or services to more specific sub-segments. Knowing the ideal personas for each relevant segment of your business is a powerful tool. It allows you to make wiser and more targeted marketing decisions and investments. Within the world of podcast interviews, for example, understanding your ideal buyer persona and developing segments for different products or services can help you better target particular content. You could share a different story that resonates with that audience, or make an offer ideal for those specific listeners, for example. Providing the correct content with the correct context to each individual interview will provide them more value and you more listeners back to your site who come eager to engage.

Who do you want to avoid speaking with?

As important is it is to look at your ideal customer, it's also important to avoid working with customers who aren't a good match for your business. These people could cost you more money than they make you. They're the dreaded nightmare customers. We all have nightmare customers from time to time. They drain our energy. They don't value our products or services. You can never make them happy and will become frustrated if you tried. The people in this category are your negative buyer personas and are to be avoided. They aren't necessarily bad people, they're just not a good fit for your businesses. It could be they don't value what you're selling for the price you're selling it for. The way we service and deliver our product may not coincide with their preference. They may be an ideal buyer persona for someone else, but not you. Let that other person have their business.

As you target your ideal buyer persona more effectively you will get to know them over time. You will even assign a name to them. You will naturally begin to recognize and talk to your ideal potential customers and distance yourself from negative buyer personas.

The truth is that we all attract nightmare or crazy customers, and it's usually our own fault. We attract nightmare or crazy customers because we market to nightmare and crazy customers. We spend time and money to connect with them. The key to reducing how many we attract is to target more effectively and intentionally and make sure that your business and message clearly demonstrate who your ideal customer is and who isn't a good fit. The responsibility is yours. Your marketing message must be clear so you attract your ideal customers but repel those who you can't serve well.

Spending a little time up front to paint a picture of your ideal customer and then targeting them, and only them, is one of the best ways to set your business up for success. A marketing campaign that attracts the right people has the best chance to produce the largest number of profitable customers.

Here is a chart of items to consider as you build your business and marketing campaign that address demographic and psychographic factors to consider. Revisit it from time to time as your business grows and you learn more about your ideal customer. This profile will be your starting point for determining which podcasts to target during your podcast guest tours.

Demographic Questions (Who my customers are):

- Age Range:
- Gender:
- Marital Status:
- Parental Status:
- Geographical Area (Urban, Suburban, Rural, States with Snow, States with ocean front, etc.):
- Education Level:
- Income Range:
- Debt Level:
- Standard of Living:
- Employment Status (Self-employed, Employee, Student, Retired):
- Employer/Company Type (Non-profit, Government, Size of Business):
- How long at current company or position:
- Occupation or Job Title:
- Sports or Activities:
- What's on their phone or radio? Podcast, music, news:
- Political leaning of affiliation:

- TV Shows, Movies and video they might watch:
- Books, magazines and blogs they might read:
- Other (Anything else specifically relevant to your niche):

Psychographic Questions (What my customers want and feel):

- What are their fears?
- What are their aspirations and dreams?
- How do they see themselves?
- How do others see them?
- How do they want others to see them?
- What do they value most?
- Why do they do what they do? (What is their core motivation?)
- How do they make decisions?
- How do they learn? (Visual, Auditory, Kinesthetic):
- Who do they respect?
- Who influences their decisions?
- Where are they on the innovation adoption curve? (Innovators, Early Adopters, Early Majority, Late Majority, Laggards):
- What do they believe about your industry? Do they assign a stereotype to it?

- What is their biggest likely objection to engaging with you?
- What would be the worst case, biggest embarrassment, for them if they with you?
- What would be the best case, biggest win, for them if they work with you?
- How will they go about making the decision to work with you?
- Other (Anything else specifically relevant to your niche):

WHERE TO FIND PODCASTS

With over 300,000 podcasts, how do you go about starting to find the small subset that is right for you? Simple. Here are five ways to get a more manageable list of perfect podcasts:

1. **Ask current (or known potential) customers:** Ask current or known potential customers if they listen to podcasts and, if so, what podcasts they listen to. Often, these are the best ones for you to be on.

2. **iTunes:** Go to iTunes and search for keywords and sort by categories. Especially when you're first starting out, look at the New and Noteworthy shows in your section. The new and noteworthy podcasts are highlighted for the first eight weeks or so. These are often shows that are up and comers and building momentum.

   I'll talk a bit more about new shows in a bit when we talk about screening podcasts after putting together your list, but the New and Noteworthy shows are often good shows to keep an eye on or reach out to. When you're first getting started, New and Noteworthy shows can be easier to land, as they're not as popular as the more seasoned shows yet, but your episode will be live for a long time, ready to benefit from their increase in popularity.

3. **Social media:** Search Facebook, Twitter, and LinkedIn for groups, posts, or hashtags, that are relevant to your brand. Include the word "podcast" and you'll likely find some shows that qualify for

further analysis. Ask questions on your accounts or in relevant groups for recommended podcasts. If you're engaging within eye-shot of your ideal customer, asking what podcasts they listen to can get some great recommendations. Go where your audience is, search, and ask questions.

4. **Competitors:** Google the name of a competitor and the word "podcast" and you may see several podcasts where they have been interviewed. You can also search for their name in iTunes as well to see if you can find an interview they did. Take advantage of their homework (subject to you confirming it's right for you, which I help you with next) and write down the relevant results. This will help show you where other people in your industry think your ideal customers are. And don't worry, you're not stealing listeners or clients from them. You're adding value to similar people. That's what business is all about. There are plenty of customers to go around.

5. **Podcast Hosts:** The podcast community is very small and intertwined, especially within industries or niches. Podcast hosts know other podcast hosts. A referral from one is a great way to get more interviews. Thus, podcast hosts are a great resource for you. Whenever you get an interview, it's best practice to ask the host at the end of the interview if there are any other podcasts that you would be a great guest on. If you can just get two referrals from every successful podcast interview, you will never have to cold call shows again. In addition to shows you have been on, or if you're just starting out, also connect with podcast hosts who you may know in different industries or niches for relevant referrals. Chances are they will know a few podcasts that will fit your business well.

Going through these five exercises will likely give you a long list of podcasts with the right general listenership to warrant your attention. These next steps, however, will help you really hone in on finding the best shows among the bunch to help you maximize the impact of your time. You will see that the rest of the system will be focusing on marketing to the correct people, not just more people, and then serving them well so they will connect with you after the show.

Action Steps:

1. Ask five current or known potential customers what podcasts they listen to.
2. Conduct five searches on iTunes for relevant podcasts.
3. Search on LinkedIn, Facebook, and Twitter (or any other social media sites that are aligned to your particular industry) for relevant podcasts.
4. Google five competitors and "podcast" to find shows they have been on.
5. Search iTunes for those competitors, too.
6. List at least five podcast hosts you know who you can ask for referrals. Don't actually ask yet. I'll turn you loose on this one once you go through the rest of the system and are ready to start being on shows because this one escalates quickly!

GETTING STARTED: TARGETING THE PERFECT PODCAST

Right now, it's estimated that over one hundred million people in the United States regularly listen to podcasts. One study done in 2016 showed that 36% of the US population had listened to podcasts and 21% listened regularly. This number is expected to rise dramatically as podcasts go from being an add-on to radio, to a replacement for radio, functioning like on-demand radio. Cars are already being equipped to download episodes directly to the dashboard. There will soon be no technological barrier to you going from obscure to acclaimed as a featured podcast guest. No longer will you need to be broadcast over the radio to connect with people on their commutes.

You don't want to be on all 300,000-plus podcasts. Even if each of them could theoretically get you in the ears or cars of consumers, not all of them are equal. Some would be a waste of time; others are goldmines. Your focus should be on the quality of people you're talking to, not necessarily the quantity. In this case, quality means people who could be an ideal customer for you, who would benefit from your unique story and expertise, and who are ready to take action and who will know right away that they want to work with you.

In fact, you might get much better traction speaking on a show with a 500-person listenership full of your ideal customers than speaking on a show with a 50,000-person listenership that has little to no connection to your services or expertise. Early on in my research I had the opportunity to appear on a very big podcast that had over 40,000 downloads per episode. It was one of my earlier experiments into maximizing the impact of being a podcast guest.

Before the interview I made sure I did everything under my control as well as I could. I followed every best practice I knew so that the only major variable would be the listenership. Although that interview makes for great conversations, some vanity numbers, as well as a valuable piece of research for my system (and anecdote for this book), out of over 40,000 downloads I received only a handful of leads.

Shortly after that interview I was accepted on another podcast. This podcast typically got only 300 downloads per episode. In fact, the host was even apologetic that her audience was that small. I assured her that my purpose in being interviewed was to provide maximum value to hand-selected audiences. I wanted to focus on a topic that would be meaningful to them. My goal was to connect to get them to know, like, and trust me and then offer services that I can help people with if they want to engage more with me. Just like with the other podcast, and every other interview I do, I prepared and made sure to do everything under my control as well as I could. That interview got me 150 leads. There is no doubt that my time was better spent talking to 300 ideal people than over 40,000 random people.

In other words, there are more fish in the ocean than there are in a barrel, but it's much easier to catch fish in a barrel. The key, therefore, becomes finding the right podcasts, which I will help you do right now.

How to qualify podcasts

In order to identify which podcasts on your list will be the highest value to your marketing campaign, we first look to qualify them to identify which ones have listeners to whom you can provide the most value. This starts with going back to the goals of your business and campaign to start matching listener qualities with your offerings and expertise. Ask yourself what you are trying to accomplish with your podcast-guest marketing. Are you looking to sell more books? Are you looking to sell other products or services? Are you looking for public speaking opportunities? Are you looking to promote a crowdfunding project?

These are all questions to ask as you qualify shows to make sure you're getting the right exposure for your goals. Exposure isn't the goal. Just getting known isn't the goal. After all, we know of people like Lee Harvey Oswald, John Wilkes Booth, and Osama Bin Laden, that becoming known doesn't necessarily mean becoming acclaimed.

To become acclaimed, keep your business and campaign goals handy and consider this five-part test to screen all podcasts:

1. **Will I be speaking to my ideal customers**? This isn't a yes or no question. There is hardly any show where one hundred percent of listeners will be your ideal customer. This can be either a percentage question or a total number question.

   If a high percentage of the audience is your ideal customer, that's great. If a lower percentage is your ideal customer, but that lower percentage is a large enough number, that may be okay as well. They key is looking into what percentage and what total number of ideal customers could be listening to the show.

2. **Has the show released at least ten episodes?** The reality is that for many of the reasons I prefer being a podcast guest over a podcast host, podcasting is a tough platform and many podcasters don't last long. In fact, a lot of podcast hosts end their show before hitting the ten episode mark. Even worse, some will record a few episodes and never release them at all. Being interviewed on these shows would be a total waste of your time. Make sure your content will be heard and promoted today and for years to come on a long running podcast.
3. **Does the show release shows on a regular basis?** Just like blogging, showing up and releasing episodes on a consistent basis is important for the long-term success of a podcast. You'll maximize the impact of your time by making sure to be on podcasts that stick to a regular schedule of posting their interviews.
4. **Is the show consistent with your brand?** Just like with your public social profiles, making sure you're on shows that are consistent with your brand, and image, is important for your long-term success because you will be judged by the company you keep. Make sure that the host, show, and anything particular to the episode, are consistent with your overall brand. For example, some shows are marked explicit in iTunes, which may not be consistent with a professional image. Hosts might curse (or may not curse, if that's your thing). Make sure each part of the show adds to your brand and image and doesn't take anything away from it.
5. **Does the podcast have show notes?** While podcasts can be found and listened to on iTunes, most

podcasters have a website too. Here listeners can listen to the podcast and also access written summaries of each episode. Often called "show notes," these blog posts typically include links back to the guest's website. Back links are gold to any website. They're signals to search engines that a particular website sees your website as a credible, authoritative source they want to direct their visitors. Major companies invest large amounts of time and money acquiring quality back links to improve their SEO (Search Engine Optimization). You will earn these powerful trust signals with every podcast interview that has show notes.

These are the five main considerations when considering whether to target or appear on a show. Yours may vary a bit. You may develop more that are important to your business, or not care as much about one or two of these for your business, however I strongly encourage you to at least consider these five items as part of your targeting and decision making process.

Action Steps:

1. Identify your test to screen podcasts down to the most relevant for your business or campaign, using my four-part test as a starting point.
2. Take your list of podcasts and run through your screening test for each of them.

PITCHING THE PODCAST HOST

Nobody likes receiving cold calls. Blind emails, in the case of most podcast pitches, are worthless, especially if the pitch emails are obviously canned messages with only the name of the podcast is changed. Those are beyond worthless and can even crush your marketing campaign before it starts. Remember, if you follow my target podcast interview marketing plan those emails to the podcast host are in reality sent to the gatekeepers to your ideal customers. A sour impression can close an important door for a long time. It can turn a host from being neutral about you and your service to someone who is negative about you and your service.

Just like physicians who take the Hippocratic Oath that states "First do no harm," so should you. These pitches are important. Be sure to do no harm by sending cold, canned emails with just the name of the podcast swapped out.

Cold calls or blind emails are what's known in the marketing world as "outbound marketing" and come across as saying "I have something to sell you," instead of "I can serve you and your listeners well." That's why my system focuses on warm introductions that provide more results in less time. Fortunately, I'm about to share three ways to warm up your introduction before ever reaching out to a podcast host. As you will see, these are built on the basis of creating value for the podcast host, first, to let them know that you're different than other guests. You want more than just access to their listeners' ears.

These ways will let the podcast know that you want to (and can) add value to them and their listeners. To supercharge your efforts, consider combining more than one of these methods, just be sure to avoid overkill.

1. **Find a common connection.** In years past, people talked about finding your six degrees of separation to another person. With all of the social networks around these days, that number has reduced to two or three degrees, tops, between you and anyone in your industry. As a result, the odds are you can find a common connection to the host. Ask your friends who host podcasts if they have a connection. If not, check social networks like LinkedIn to see who you know who may be connected with the host. Facebook is useful for this purpose, too, because you can see whether you have common Facebook friends and can search industry Facebook groups you participate in to see if they're a member as well.

2. **Get on their radar by giving, giving, and giving some more**. Nick Pavlidis, of Confessions of a Terrible Husband: Lessons Learned from a Lumpy Couch, talks about connecting with influencers by giving value over time before asking for anything in return. For example, Nick was heavily influenced by Dan Miller, author of 48 Days to the Word You Love, John G. Miller, author of QBQ! The Question Behind the Question, Fawn Weaver, author of The Happy Wives Club, Gretchen Ruben, author of Happier at Home, and several other bestselling authors, as he began improving his relationship and building his brand.

   When he started blogging and planning his podcast, he made sure he commented on and shared nearly all of those influencers' blog posts and podcast episodes as they were released. He engaged with them on social media, wrote and spoke about their influence, and let them know when he mentioned them on his blog or in social media by tagging them in the posts. He made it very clear to them that he appreciated their content and was there to help them reach more people.

He also helped with product launches, such as Fawn Weaver's book launch and Gretchen Ruben's latest book, and attended events where they were speaking to support them. Although this may seem like a lot of work, Nick was reading their content anyhow, so leaving a thoughtful comment or sharing a post on social media required a mere seconds more than he was already doing.

When it was time to launch his podcast, he sent personal emails to each of these people asking them if they would be willing to be a guest on his show. You probably don't need me to tell you, but by that point, Nick had provided great value to them, not expecting anything in return, but they certainly knew Nick as a giver and someone who added value to them. His email request was also completely customized to let them know that their content added value to his marriage and he wanted to help them expand their audience by sharing their expertise on his show. If you want to see how effective Nick's give-first system is, you can just check his episode list for the names I just mentioned.

The same can be true to be featured as a guest on a show. Many podcasters don't get a lot of comments or shares on their show notes, especially shows with smaller, but heavily–niched audiences. An easy way for you to stand out is to engage with them on the show notes and share their posts. Most podcasters will get an email notification to tell them that someone commented on their post. Those notifications are very exciting for podcasters and bloggers. When they open that email and see that it was you and then read your thoughtful comment, they will associate you with that happiness. When it comes to social media sharing, be sure to include their handle/username when you share their post for social media platforms that allow that, like Twitter and Facebook, so they get notified that you are sharing their content.

3. **Review their podcast and then supercharge that review.** Even the most popular podcasts get very few reviews, especially from people who aren't other podcasters, yet reviews are one of the most valuable aspects in getting shows noticed and encouraging people to click play. Podcasters know that. Because of that, you can stand out in the crowd by giving a review on iTunes, Stitcher, or other podcast delivery apps that allow reviews.

   Unlike blog comments or social media mentions, hosts aren't automatically notified when someone leaves a review, however they do check. In fact, many of them read positive reviews on the air of their shows.

   You're going to make sure you stand out from the crowd by first making sure your screen name when submitting a review lets them know it's you by either using your name and brand name or your full name. Then, you're going to super charge the value you add for them by taking a screen shot of your review and then sharing your screen shot on social media with a message encouraging others to listen to that show and tagging the host so they see it. Don't worry, taking a screen shot is easy. To make it even easier for you, I include a tutorial on how to leave a review and then take a screen shot of it on the resources page at www.PodcastGuestProfits.com/Resources.

Each of these methods shows the podcaster that you're someone who adds value first and warms up your introduction before you send it. Now that the introduction is warmed up, it's important that the introduction makes it easy for them to say yes by communicating effectively.

COMMUNICATING EFFECTIVELY WITH THE PODCAST HOST

One thing to note about communicating with podcasters is that the most effective communication isn't necessarily e-mail. The one that works best and easiest often depends on your circumstances and that of the decision maker at the podcast. Communication can include LinkedIn messages, social media conversations, forums on their website or another website, in person at events, regular mail, postcards, or by sending a gift with a note. The list is only limited by your imagination.

For this example we'll use e-mail because it's the most common method of connecting with podcasters. The same principles can be applied to whichever medium best fits your circumstances, however. Specifically, any effective communication needs to include the following elements.

1. **Context and customization.** No matter what form you use, make sure that you have context, meaning that the message you communicate is specific to the host's needs and his or her podcast. If you are doing your outreach yourself, listen to at least a few shows to get a sense of their focus, flow, and format. If you are outsourcing this, make sure whoever is doing your outreach does this. As you or your representatives learn about their audience it would be wise to show the host specifically how you would add value to their show.

2. **Be concise.** Podcasters are busy. Make sure the subject line of any e-mail shows them that you will offer something valuable for their listeners. Something to the effect of "complimentary book for your listeners" or "complimentary resource for your listeners" can tell them right away that you're going to offer value. Avoid the word "free" as this typically is a signal to spam filters. Of course, you have to be ready to follow through on any promise you make, which we will talk about in detail in Section Two.

   No matter what medium you choose, get to the point quick. Show them within the first one hundred words that you have something valuable to offer their audience, are familiar with their show, are an expert, and will be a professional interview. Make it easy for them to say yes. Your communication should tell them that you will be the easiest guest to work with and high value to their audience.

3. **Position yourself as a professional.** You'll want to link to your experience with previous podcasts or speeches. In fact, if you have appeared on several other podcasts, you can consider having them on all one page on your website, so they can see that their show will be added there as well for continuing cross promotion. Also, acknowledge the equipment you have so that they know you will sound just as good as them. We will talk about equipment later, but you can find recommended setups starting well less than $100.00 on the resources page at www.PodcastGuestProfits.com/Resources.

4. **Let them know you will help promote the episode.** Make sure that you acknowledge that you'll promote the episode on your social media just as hard as they will on theirs. If you have a large reach, let them know

that. If you use social media sharing systems like Meet Edgar, which you can find on the resources page and lets you schedule posts to automatically repost over and over again, let them know. This tells them you aren't just looking to get something, but are willing to give over and over again.

5. **Include a testimonial or two.** If you have a customer or connection who would be influential to the podcaster, you could mention it in your communication to them. A testimonial from another podcaster could be helpful to let them know you're easy to work with and a great promoter, for example.

Supercharge your Communication with a Perfect Pitch Sheet

If you want to take your communication up a notch, I strongly suggest creating a one-page document that includes the items we just talked about and positions you as a professional. Having a professional-looking pitch sheet can be the critical piece that introduces you. It makes a professional first impression and establishes you as an expert guest they need to share with their listeners. Don't worry, making sure your pitch sheet is perfectly prepared to make a professional first impression is simpler than you think. Here are eight steps to the perfect pitch sheet. You can also find step-by-step instructions on the resources page.

1. **A logo.** A simple logo that is clear and consistent with your marketing campaign is critical. A professional logo helps build trust with listeners and will become important when we talk about preparing for and conducting effective interviews that turn listeners into leads. A quality logo doesn't have to cost a lot of money either. If you don't already have one, I have

included several places where you can get an affordable, quality logo created on the resources page.

2. **A memorable tag line.** A tag line in this context is one short sentence that shows the host why they should have you on their show. It isn't necessarily your company tag line, but a short statement that helps the host justify giving you valuable access to his audience. It answers the big question, "What do you bring to this show?"

3. **A professional image.** Include a professional image of you that is consistent with your brand. The image could be the same image you use on your Twitter and LinkedIn profiles, if they look for more information. Consistency and professionalism are important to building trust and authority as an expert. Remember everything should be build trust and authority. This image you provide will likely be used in the show notes and social media posts to promote the podcast.

   Don't worry, a professional image doesn't need to involve a full-day photo session or cost hundreds of dollars. Simple, but professional is what we aim for here. Some of the best ones I've ever seen have come from Sears or J.C. Penney photo shops for less than $100. In fact, as of this writing Groupon.com almost always has a J.C. Penny deal that offers you one professional photography shoot with a three-image digital album and one traditional print for only $29.99. That will give you everything you need.

4. **Background information.** Tell the host very quickly who you are and what you offer their audience. Remember, they're putting their trust and credibility with their audience on the line every time they share the mic with someone. Make sure you include a short

biographical statement to let them know you're a professional and will respect that trust.

5. **Discussion topics.** Include a few relevant topics to their show that overlap with your expertise. You may also include one or two references to great blogs, interviews, videos or other compelling content that has context to their audience. More isn't always better. Focus and make sure to reference no more than four of the best and relevant topics and stories that you have. As you prepare for your campaign you will want to have a valuable free offer to provide listeners so they can connect with you, so be sure to pick topics on which you can prepare or already have a free resource to promote as a call to action at the end of the interview.

6. **Professional biography**. This is a short paragraph that host will likely read to introduce you. Make sure it's in the third person, so it can be read by the host. Keep it between fifty and one hundred words and don't be humble. Make it an introduction your biggest fan would give you. When listeners hear a host they trust say those nice things about you it will help you establish a stronger connection from the start.

7. **Contact information.** Make it easy for the host to book you for their show. Include links to your social media accounts and, especially, your LinkedIn profile. Make it easy for them to connect. Include your email address, cell phone number, a Skype address (many interviews occur over Skype), and a link to a calendar scheduler so they can get right on your calendar to schedule an appointment. This last part is key, as it allows you to control the times you're interviewed even though you're reaching out. It also makes it simple to schedule a time with you, so nobody needs to go back and forth with emails. There are several

free and paid services that give you this functionality in a matter of minutes, like Time Trade, Calendly, or ScheduleOnce.com. I have listed several more in the resources page, including tutorials on how to set up my favorite three.

8. **A testimonial.** The most effective testimonials for this section will focus on you as a guest and professional. It should talk about you being knowledgeable, entertaining, energetic, and informative. This isn't a business testimonial. The goal is to tell the host that you will be a great guest. The more relevant the person providing the testimonial is to the subject matter of show, the better. Many guests will have multiple pitch sheets on different topics or the same pitch sheet with different testimonials. They decide which ones to send out based on the host and audience. If you want to supercharge the testimonial, take a look at their former guests or someone they know. Check their LinkedIn profile. Do you have already have a mutual connection? If so, make sure to use those. Include a picture of the person giving the testimonial. That way, if they're just skimming the sheet they might see a face that they recognize and trust, even if that face isn't yours.

   I suggest you do make multiple versions of the sheet, switching out the topics, testimonial, and other content to fit the particular podcasts you're focusing on. When I first started, I had three different sheets, each with slightly different talking points and a different recommendation from someone noted in that particular field. One sheet focused on ecommerce and included a testimonial from Alaa Hassan, a noted speaker. Another sheet focused on inbound marketing and included a testimonial from Sam

Mallikarjunan, the director of Inbound.org. The third focused on entrepreneurial podcasts and included a testimonial from Dan Miller, author of *48 Days to the Work You Love*.

Each of them was focused on my expertise, although each of them were even more focused on a subset of my offerings based on what would serve the specific podcast. Remember that content is king, but context is god. Having multiple versions of the one-sheet that each present within a context that is relevant to the specific podcast will help you connect more effectively with each host. Here is an example of one of my current pitch sheets.

<<{insert image sheet}>>

Keep at it

Finally, it's important to remember that no matter what way you communicate, or how great your pitch sheet is, one contact may not be enough. Be persistent and conscious that one method of communication may be more effective with a particular host. Albert Einstein said the definition of insanity was doing the same thing and expecting different results. It applies to this system of targeted podcast interview marketing. You may need to reach out multiple times (each time with a different, custom message) or in multiple ways, to connect with the host.

One email may not be enough to get on their radar, although using my method of warming up the introduction will certainly help you. In sales, it's often said sales are only made after seven contacts. This may be excessive for being a podcast guest, but the point is that the better your relationship with the podcaster is, the more likely it is that you will be accepted on their show.

Be creative and use multiple methods to add value to them and have them get to know you. Here are a few other suggestions for standing out:

1. **Every time you see them at a conference, introduce yourself.** Ask about being a guest.
2. **If you have a book or any printed material, send them the book.** Even if they don't read it, they will see you as an expert, a giver, and a professional. In fact, multiple studies show that, on average, people respect published authors more than they do those with a Ph.D.
3. **Go old school to get on the radar screen, sending a handwritten note.**
4. **Get creative.** The best pitch I have ever seen came along with a gum ball machine. Matt Miller of School Spirit Vending got a major host's attention by sending them a gum ball machine personalized with their podcast's art work. This out-of-the-box thinking started a conversation and led to the opportunity for Matt to speak to over 350,000 of his ideal customers.

Sometimes you will find out that a podcaster uses a third-party gatekeeper. When this happens, just use the same techniques. Be respectful and focus on what's in it for them and their audience. People are people and gatekeepers share the same concerns as the podcaster, albeit with one added caveat. Ultimately, the gatekeeper or the producer of the show wants to look like a genius for having you on. Make it easy for them.

Getting on your first half dozen podcasts can be a challenge. The hardest part is the first ninety days. You will begin to build confidence and momentum with every pitch and every interview. Trust the proven system. If you continue to work through this system and focus on getting invited onto (or referred to) at least two additional podcasts after each interview, you will have more opportunities than you have time for the interviews.

Action Steps:

1. Identify at least five podcasters who you want to connect with whom you don't already have a relationship.
2. Start commenting, sharing content, and reviewing their podcasts.
3. Reach out to at least three people who are relevant to your industry and niche and ask if they will give you a testimonial.
4. If you don't have a logo, get one created. If you need help finding an affordable place to get a quality logo, head over to the resources page for several suggestions.
5. If you don't have a recent, professional image, get one taken.

POSITIONING YOURSELF AS AN EXPERT

Why would anyone want to hear you? That is a vital question that you must ask yourself and be able to confidently answer to position yourself as an expert. Many people struggle with this. Don't worry, though. I can help you with that.

The good news is that you already have a lot of the answer figured out. Having defined who you want to talk to is a necessary first step to connecting with them in a way that will serve them. At the same time, you will be letting them know that you're the person they should turn to for help. People want to listen to experts. In fact, they tune into podcasts to find helpful information or inspiration, so they're there ready to be helped. They will engage with you once they hear you sincerely helping them with a problem they already know they have, which makes getting the right message to the right podcasts even more effective.

Podcast hosts also need interesting guests with valuable information to share. Interview-based shows depend on quality guests to provide content to their audience. Jay Leno and Johnny Carson needed great guests. So do most podcast hosts. They need good guests as much as you need good exposure. Positioning yourself right will show those hosts that they can trust an episode to you. Hosts are looking to book interesting and credible thought leaders. They want experts who can share quality information and entertaining stories to keep their listeners' attention. Hosts want to provide information that positively impacts their listeners, moving them forward in a way that is meaningful to their lives. Every host wants the best thought leaders and authority makers.

Do you see yourself as an in-demand expert? Most people don't. If not, don't worry. By the end of this chapter you will know exactly how to position yourself to make the right connections.

Most people's biggest struggle isn't that they have nothing worthwhile to say. To the contrary, most people's struggle is that they don't believe they have something worthwhile to say. They feel the pressure that in order to be an expert they need to be the expert, instead of an expert. They ask themselves, "Why would anyone want to hear me, when they could go buy a book for twenty-five dollars on the same topic that has sold three million copies?" They wonder why anyone would listen to their financial advice when they can go buy Dave Ramsey's My Total Money Makeover, for example. They see other "experts" in their topics who have been active for years and think there is no room for them. Nothing could be further from the truth.

The fact is that all of us are experts in some area of business or life. You're an expert if you work sixty hours a week in your field and have done so for at least two or three years, you've founded a company (that succeeded or failed), you've written a book, and more, which I will discuss below.

You're also the expert in two very important categories: your life story and your opinion. Being an expert in an area relevant to your business and the expert on your story and opinion is the foundation needed to start a successful campaign as a podcast guest. Every day, thousands of people consume financial advice not given by Dave Ramsey, Suze Orman, or David Bach. People consume business content not created by Warren Buffett, Jack Welch, or Sheryl Sandberg. People consume marriage content not written by John Gray, Dr. Laura, or Dr. Gary Chapman. There is plenty of room for you. The world needs your voice and your unique view.

If you're struggling with calling yourself an expert right now, don't worry. I can help you with that. I can help you find the expertise within you and help you confidently position yourself in a way that is consistent with your personality and knowledge. On the other hand, if your struggle is narrowing down your expertise to just one or two topics, I can help, too, because in many ways being an expert on everything can be more harmful to your marketing than not seeing your expertise at all. People can perceive you as overconfident or even pompous. Know-it-alls don't connect with or relate to the average listener. As comedian, author, and speaker Ken Davis says "nothing will destroy your relationship faster than trying to portray a sense of perfection". If you act like you know everything about everything, you aren't seen as an expert but a fool. It will water down your credibility as an expert on the topics that are core to your business.

When I first started as a podcast guest, my struggle was with the concept of being the expert. If that's your struggle, too, you're in good company. It's a good and healthy place to start. I had a hard time calling myself an expert at anything until a friend who is a lawyer shared the definition of an expert witness in the legal context.

An expert witness, he explained, is someone who by virtue of their education, training, skill, or experience is believed to have expertise or specialized knowledge in a particular subject beyond that of the average person.

After letting that definition sink in, the weight of being the expert lifted, especially with respect to business management and marketing, topics in which I had all of the expert indicators that courts believe are worthy when asking for outside subject matter advice. I no longer felt like I needed to be the one and only undisputed expert, but found confidence in being an expert in business, systems, and marketing because I have education, training, skill, experience, and relevant knowledge that goes well beyond that of the average person and many self described experts.

I've broken down the definition and shared some examples. This should help you find your expertise so you can confidently and honestly position yourself as an expert:

By virtue of their education

Dr. Phil Carson is a licensed pharmacist. He's an expert and a great podcast guest. Lawyers, doctors, architects, engineers, nurses, and countless other professionals are experts because they have significant formal education in their field. Do you have formal education in your field that can position you as an expert?

By virtue of their skill

Carrie Wilkerson, The Barefoot Executive is an online business expert. She is a sought-after guest appearing on national radio, TV, and some of the biggest podcasts, yet she never graduated from college. Her expertise comes from the skills she learned building a multimillion dollar business all while being a wife and mother. Self-taught artists, musicians, or athletes, and others are experts in their field because of what they can do or have done. Their expertise doesn't come from any official degree or certification they obtained. What skills do you have that you can confidently each to others?

By virtue of their training

The distinction between training, education, and experience is sometimes subtle. For example, the difference between experts by training compared to experts by education is generally that training is skill-specific teachings compared to more knowledge-based teachings within a formal education system for experts by education. Experts by training don't necessarily have a formal education or degree in their area, but do have skill-specific training.

The difference between experts by training and experts by experience is that experts by experience is that an expert by experience may not have any formal education or skill-specific training, but they have been doing something long enough that they become more skilled than the average person.

Josh Brown is the expert in setting up and buying a franchise. While Josh is a licensed lawyer, his years of study and training working specifically in franchise law have made him the expert in this niche. In what specific areas have you trained and achieved a level of knowledge you can confidently share with others?

By virtue of their experience:

Aaron Walker is an expert entrepreneur based on over three decades in business growth and ownership. Although he doesn't have a formal business degree or specific trainings in operation, he successfully operated and sold eight businesses in the last thirty years. In what areas relevant to your business do you have experience from which you can confidently teach others?

Believed to have expertise or specialized knowledge in a particular subject beyond that of the average person

If you have been through a formal education, extended training, have a unique skill, or have years of experience, chances are there are topics or even narrow subtopics in which you have knowledge beyond that of an average person. There are probably many people who could learn from you. The difference between those who make progress as experts and those who don't, however, is often their confidence level. While you never want to misrepresent yourself, it's important that you recognize that you have the ability to help others with what you know.

In preparing for using podcast guest appearances to connect with listeners, it's important that you identify the areas where you can confidently position yourself as someone who has the knowledge and ability to help. If not, the host will know it, the audience will feel it, and your momentum and connection will suffer. As such, it's important to make sure that you identify your areas of expertise and confidence as you prepare for your podcast interviews, so you can position yourself to help and be perceived as helpful.

Most hosts will not do an extensive background check to verify your credentials. Instead they most likely will turn to the web to corroborate what you presented in your pitch. They will search for you on the web to see if your website, LinkedIn profile, and social media profiles are consistent with your story and expertise. Some hosts may even ask for a pre-interview discussion to get to know you and get a feel of how well you present yourself and that you know your stuff.

To recap, the best way to position yourself for an effective podcast guest tour is to be able to identify the areas where you can confidently position yourself as an expert and add unique value. The most effective way to do so is to share specialized knowledge (the generalist isn't an expert; the person who focuses, who specializes can be) in a particular subject (the most effective interview is where you talk just about the topics connected to your expertise and business), that are beyond that of an average person (that average person is the host and listener who are looking to improve in that particular area). In fact, when you're sharing your expertise as an expert, you will be speaking with a number of experts on other topics, who are average when it comes to your topic.

What type of expert are you?

Now that we have discussed how you acquired your expertise (i.e. through education, skill, training, or experience), it's important to identify what type of expert you will be. Another way to think of this is with what expert voice you speak as you teach others. There are three basic types of experts, or expert voices, you might be: the Scholar, the Sherpa, and the Traveler. Any of these experts can use podcast guest appearances to build their brand and speak to their audience in a way that encourages the listeners to engage with you.

The Scholar

The Scholar is an expert who's studied the subject and been awarded advanced degrees. Often, people who become experts by education choose to speak as a Scholar in their marketing, especially when marketing to peers in the same industry. The Scholar has written and lectured about the subject in levels far above what the average person understands. Often the Scholar has a title and initials behind their name, such as Doctor, Reverend, Professor, or Ph.D.

The Scholar voice involves speaking with great authority. The Scholar is there to teach. They don't always use a professorial voice, if that isn't their natural tone, but they confidently speak in their own voice in a way to let them know that the Scholar is there to teach. It can be more of a lecture than a discussion. They often use research, statistics, and tested theories to share their knowledge and connect with listeners.

John Johnson, PhD, is a great podcast guest and example of a Scholar expert. Dr. Johnson is a noted economist who completed his doctoral training at MIT, one of the most prestigious and respected schools in his field. The courts look to him to explain what data means in some of the largest anti-trust cases, class action suits, and trials where hundreds of millions of dollars are at stake. Dr. Johnson can explain to juries what the confusing data means and doesn't mean. As an author, he uses this unique expertise in his book *EVERYDATA: The Misinformation Hidden in the Little Data You Consume Every Day*. As a highly sought after podcast guest he uses it to explain the data the specific audience sees every day. He instructs them on how to make better decisions.

The Sherpa

The Sherpa has traveled the path on which his customers are traveling successfully. The Sherpa is there to show you the way and can tell you the pitfalls and shortcuts. The Sherpa is your expert guide who can tell you what your next step should be because they have already taken it. They're sometimes called the veteran, the old timer, or the wise sage. While the Scholar teaches through statistics and study, the Sherpa teaches through experience and personally-gathered wisdom.

Robert Mallon and Bill Watkins of the Rusty Lion Academy are expert entrepreneurs and business leaders. They have started, grown, and sold businesses. They have held leadership positions in large well-known and respected companies. They have been top performers in sports, business, and their community. At home, they have also been top performers as husbands and fathers. Robert and Bill draw on a combined eight decades of experience to bring a wealth of information, knowledge, and wisdom you can't get from any degree. Robert and Bill are Sherpas that hosts and listeners love to hear.

The Traveler

Travelers are people going through the journey with you. Traveler don't have decades of success or multiple degrees in their area of expertise, but they're teachers at heart and have an innate way to share struggles, lessons, and resources with others as they work towards the same result. Travelers share insights, struggles, failures, and successes. Travelers are often the easiest type of expert voice for listeners to relate to because there is no doubt that they understand the struggles and goals of the listener.

Nick Pavlidis, author of the book *Confessions of a Terrible Husband: Lessons Learned from a Lumpy Couch,* and host of a podcast by the same name, is looked at as an expert in marriage and family relationships. You might wonder how a self-proclaimed terrible husband could be seen an expert in the very topic he claims to be terrible at.

If you have heard Nick speak or read his material, you would see how well he understands the struggles of men trying to juggle business, family, and personal goals. You would think that he's been spying on you and reading your mind. Nick is the prototypical Traveler and proud of it. He even choose a brand name to let you know exactly what he's there to do. Listeners hear Nick tell his story and share his struggles and insights. They immediately feel empowered to do the same. Listeners leave with more information and motivation to improve their relationships at home. He brings a level of camaraderie and connection that neither the Scholar nor the Sherpa could.

We're all experts in at least one area. As I mentioned above, we're all the experts in two areas. Many people are experts in several areas, Scholars in some, Sherpas in others, and Travelers in others still. A lawyer may be a Scholar in the law, a Sherpa in marketing and networking, having spent years growing a network for business and personal growth, and a Traveler in other areas of interest in which they struggle. In fact, that last sentence describes Nick Pavlidis perfectly. A lawyer by trade, Nick built a large personal network over the course of a decade but struggled at home and is on a mission to change that.

As you prepare your marketing campaign it's important to identify your expertise, how it was acquired and with what expert voice you will confidently and honestly speak so you can target the shows and hosts who connect with that voice on that subject matter.

Let's return to focus on why we're on this journey again. We're using podcast appearances to grow our band and our business. We're attempting to position ourselves as an expert, a thought leader. Our goal is for the listener to get to know, like, and trust us during the interview. We want to help the listener with our product of service. We want to have them go from listener to customer and reward us with "Certificates of Appreciation" as Rabbi Daniel Lapin describes what they give us in exchange for our help. In the United States at least, these certificates are green and have pictures of dead presidents on them.

How to deliver your knowledge so people will want to connect further with you.

As we try to sell our expertise, it's important to remember this lesson from basic sales training:

Facts tell. Stories sell.

On podcasts, no matter what kind of expert you are, and no matter how you became an expert one fact will be true: The more relevant stories you tell, the more listeners you will sell. It's that simple. Sharing your expertise through story-driven duologue connects with listeners. They get and remain engaged. They can picture the story. Stories are what they will remember. This is especially important for audio-only podcasts where you can't supplement your knowledge with graphics. The more you can share your expertise in memorable stories that have specific context to the audience, the more they will resonate with the listeners. Listeners will appreciate that you understand them. They will feel that you empathize with them. They will know that you're the person to help them solve their problems.

Without stories, you will still seem like an expert. The risk is that your interview and the knowledge you share will feel theoretical or impractical. You would be wise to identify several stories from your personal or professional experiences that demonstrate your knowledge and connection to your ideal customer before putting together your marketing plan. Better yet, practice telling those stories to friends, colleagues, or other small groups will gain you invaluable feedback and practice.

Does your public profile confirm, enhance, or take away from your expertise?

One of the biggest mistakes people make when branding themselves as an expert isn't matching their public profiles with their marketing plan. Selfies from your college days, unprofessional images or postings, and other public displays that are inconsistent with positioning you as an expert can hurt you twice. The hosts will do research when you ask to be on their show. The listeners will do research before engaging more with you. Be sure to keep your public profiles professional and consistent.

Action Steps:

1. Answer these questions to help you begin to formulate your expert profile:
    - What kind of expert are you? (Scholar, Sherpa, Traveler)
    - How did you gain your expertise? (Education, Training, Skill, Experience)
    - What particular subject is your expertise?
    - What stories do you have to support you as an expert?
    - Does your public profile on the web support your expert claim?

2. Write a fifty-word introduction as an expert you feel confident in sharing with the host, listeners, friends, and family, in the following general format:

   - I am __________ who helps ____________ so that they can ________________.

     Example, for Tom Schwab: I am a teacher, speaker, and author who helps brands go from being obscure to acclaimed through podcast interviews so that they can grow their business, sell more products or services, and increase their profits.

3. Check your public profiles on social sites like Facebook, Twitter, LinkedIn, and Instagram. Are there any that you need to protect? Any content you should add or remove? Any that need to be deleted entirely?

YOUR PROFESSIONAL PODCASTING EQUIPMENT

The last thing you need to be sure of before your campaign starts is that your equipment is set up for a quality recording. Because resources are constantly updated, I have included a guide to podcast equipment on the resources page. In short, though, you will basically need three things: microphones, headphones, and a webcam. You'll never want to use the microphone built into your computer. It will make you sound tinny, pick up background noises, and take away from your expertise because people will judge the quality of your information based on the quality of your sound. You wouldn't show up for a TV interview not looking your best. Don't show up for an audio interview not sounding your best. The host and listeners will notice. How you sound will make the first impression. Make sure you take the extra step to impress them by using a high quality microphone. When I first started, I used the iPhone earbuds that came with my iPhone, which is a huge upgrade over your computer's internal microphone, as long as you ensure that the microphone doesn't bounce back and forth on your shirt.

With even a minimum amount of cost, you can upgrade to a headset with a microphone that can plug right into your computer through a USB connection. I like this option because many have a switch built in where you can mute yourself. This can be very important if there's a background noise or if you have to clear your throat. A decent headset microphone can run between $29 and $40.

To sound like a true professional, you'll want to use the same equipment that most podcasters use. Fortunately, the cost to do so has dropped dramatically. For about $350.00, you can buy a complete Heil PR-40 microphone setup with the boom, pop shield, microphone, and cable. This will be the best of the best. The downside is this often has to be set up at one computer and can't be taken from place to place. You could also look for a happy medium setup with the Audio-Technica ATR2100-USB Cardioid Dynamic USB/XLR Microphone, for around $60 online. This will ensure you sound fantastic, as it's used by many podcasters, and is more portable than the Heil PR-40.

You could also buy an external cough switch, which is an inline switch with one button that allows you to cut your audio very easily. This allows you to take a sip of water, cough, or clear your throat without being heard. While all of this can be done in editing the burden goes on the host. As a guest you're asking the host to do it. You hope and assume they will. Just remember, if the host misses your mistake, you're the one that will end up sounding unprofessional, not them.

Besides the audio-setup, a standard set of headphones and your computer's built-in webcam fill out the basics. Some podcasts record the audio and video. You will want to sound and look your best. You can upgrade the built in computer webcam to a high-quality Logitech for as little as $50. Although the camera isn't as necessary as an upgraded microphone, it's a high-quality upgrade that you can use to record great video for additional promotion and content generation.

Although most interviews are audio-only, an increased number of shows are also recording and using the video also. You should always assume it will also have video. Make sure you have the proper backlighting, professional clothes (at least above the waist!), and a decent background. This keeps from any embarrassing surprises.

Action Step:

Head on over to the resources page at www.PodcastGuestProfits.com/Resources and either order one of the Podcast Equipment Bundles we have listed there or download the Podcast Equipment Checklist and purchase at least one of the quality USB microphones for you to make sure you have high-quality audio to match your high quality content.

SECRETS OF THE PERFECT INTERVIEW

By this point you have identified several great podcasts for you to target, added value to and started building relationships with the hosts of those shows, showing them that you can add great value to their audience, have a perfect pitch sheet (or two or three), and have the right equipment. Now you're ready to start booking shows.

If you have done the exercises leading up to this point you're ready to conduct the perfect interview and create massive value to turn listeners into leads. This section helps you do just that. By the end of this section you will be ready to talk to tens of thousands of you ideal customers, mesmerize them, and engage with them so they see you as someone they know, like, and trust. This will also help you make sure those who could be your ideal customers see you as someone who could help them solve their problem.

This isn't magic. This is a process, a marketing machine that we're building so that you can systematically succeed on each and every podcast you appear on, from your very first interview to the time you will do five interviews in one day. If you haven't done the exercises to this point I encourage you to go back and put that important foundation in place. If you have already done so, you're ready to go "on stage" and talk to your ideal customers. Let's move ahead.

American educator, author, businessman, and keynote speaker, Dr. Stephen Covey, is perhaps best known for advocating that you begin everything you do with the end in mind. In the context of *Podcast Guest Profits,* the end goal for your interviews to have the most effective long-term benefit for your business is to drive qualified visitors to your website, where you can then lead them to engaging deeper with you and forming a longer-term relationship. For the interview, however, the singular focus is to get them to your website, getting them to go from listeners to visitors.

Although not your primary goal, it's important that your interview is done in a way that makes the host look like a genius for having you on because you have massive value to offer the listeners during and after the interview. Gary Vaynerchuk talks about this as marketing with a "jab, jab, jab, right hook" strategy in his book by the same name. The jab, jab, jab, right hook strategy means that you repeatedly offer great value to an audience before you ask them to do something for you. I like to think of being a podcast guest as serve, serve, serve, ask. Only after you repeatedly serve the host and listeners will you have earned the right to ask them for something. Your podcast interview is your first opportunity to serve.

Although it isn't the goal of your interview, a frequent side effect of going through my system is to be invited back on podcasts for additional interviews or referred to other relevant podcasts. Aaron Walker, for example, was invited back to one of the most successful podcasts, *Entrepreneur on Fire,* with John Lee Dumas, for a second and third time after he masterfully followed this system. *Entrepreneur on Fire's* listeners are his ideal customers. He connects well with them, as a result of that fit. He has additional value for them on his website after the show. And he nurtures them well once they get to his site. He also secured other podcast interviews from people hearing him serve on *Entrepreneur on Fire* and based on referrals from John Lee Dumas.

If you want to conduct a perfect podcast interview each and every time, it's not magic or art. It's the system. I have designed this system based on nearly one hundred clients and over three thousand interviews. The system you're using has been adjusted, tested, and adjusted again, until it was perfected and put in an easy-to-follow format. Even better, I have included the perfect podcast interview checklist on the resources page at www.PodcastGuestProfits.com/Resources.

They say that checklists are written in blood. It's the blood of others who have made mistakes that you need not repeat. Learning from your own mistakes is painful and costly. Follow the checklist and ensure every interview is perfect. I require all of my one-on-one Interview Valet clients to have a copy of the checklist with them during every interview and highly suggest you do as well. Just head on over to the resources page and print out the most-recently-updated checklist.

I will walk you through the most important parts of the perfect podcast interview right now. After all, you may only be investing thirty minutes to any one interview, but that interview is your one chance to connect with that host and those listeners. It's critical that you have everything set before the interview so that you turn those listeners into leads.

A Week Before the Interview

Well before the interview even starts, it's important to take care of any coordination or paperwork so that when they day comes the only thing you need to worry about is your connection with the host and the content. The first thing to do is to make sure you and the host both have the interview time on your calendars. Most hosts will have a schedule manager like the ones we talked about earlier. Either way, make sure the interview is in your calendar and, if you don't schedule through the host's calendar, send an appointment invitation to the host.

The next thing you will want to do is to connect with the host on whatever platform the interview will be recorded on. If it will be recorded on Skype, send a connection request with a note that you're looking forward to the interview (and include the interview day and time, with the time zone in case you're in different time zones).

Take care of any paperwork or requests from the host as soon as possible. Some hosts will send legal releases. Although it's rare, hosts may want to make sure they have the right to use the interview. Although the industry has operated in such a way that both the host and the interviewee can use the interview content, some hosts want to make sure they have it covered in writing. If they send a legal release, read through it and check with an attorney if you have any questions.

The Day of the Interview

When the day comes, make sure to tweet out with the host's name something like: "I'm so looking forward to my interview today with @tmschwab." Everyone listens for and loves their own name. This will be a reminder to them that you're ready.

Fifteen minutes before the interview, go to a nice quiet place where you will do the recording. Make sure you turn off all the fans and computer and phone notifications, so there are no unnecessary pings or background noises. Not only is that professional courtesy, but having alerts or background noise can distract listeners from focusing on the value you provide.

Let everyone in the area know that you're being interviewed. At the office, I put a sign outside my door that says "On a recorded interview. Please do not disturb." At home, the family knows that if the office doors are closed, Dad's most likely recording and they need to be quiet.

Ten minutes before the interview, restart your computer, close out of all windows except for what you need for the recording, the host's LinkedIn profile, and the podcast's website. These are important reminders so that you can use the host's name and podcast name as you're speaking. This helps you form better connections with the host and listeners. While this may not seem necessary on your first interview, that day that you have five interviews, you will need this reminder to avoid a very embarrassing mistake. Nothing turns off a host or listener more than calling them the wrong name or not knowing the correct name of the podcast. Get a glass of water or two and get comfortable. This is going to be fun!

In addition to not wanting any unnecessary noises, you will want to close out of or eliminate anything that will take up unnecessary internet bandwidth. This could include other people at home downloading or uploading videos. For me it was once my Dropbox folder updating when a team member uploaded a new video. (Yes, much of the perfect interview checklist I urge you to use is written in *my* blood) Recording podcasts, especially if it includes video, can take up a lot of bandwidth and anything that competes with it can make Skype skip or crash, resulting in an interruption or distraction. Avoid connecting over a Wi-Fi signal if at all possible. A hardwired connection to the internet will always give you the best and most reliable connection.

Five minutes before the interview, send a Skype message to the host saying, "I'm ready and excited to go." This will show them that you're ready and cut down the nerves for both of you. If you're using another platform, a text message might be appropriate to accomplish the same thing.

During the interview

If you've prepared and gone through your pre-interview checklist, you have no reason to worry or be nervous about the interview because all of the hard work is done. Now is the time to relax and impress the host and the listeners.

For your purposes the interview starts the second you and the host are on the line together. For platforms like live streaming or live radio interviews, that's technically true. For calls made on Skype or Zoom, the host may have their settings automatically record the calls, although it isn't built into the platform automatically. Either way, always assume you're being recorded the second the connection is live. I have been surprised several times to hear what I or my clients thought was small talk before the interview makes its way to the episode.

Once you get on the line, you can stand out by offering to do a backup recording on your end. While it's rare that a recording is lost, it does happen, and neither you nor the host will want to lose a great episode. There are several programs that can help you do this easily, with new and improved ones being released all the time. Pamela on PC or eCamm Call Recorder for Mac are two well-known examples of recording software. Check the resources page for more suggestions. Offering a backup recording allows for redundancy in case the host loses the recording. You can sound like a true professional and a hero by coming up with the recording. One of our clients at Interview Valet, Chris McCluskey of Professional Christian Coaching Institute, became such a hero when he saved both his valuable time and that of the host when a recording was lost and he had a backup.

Once the interview portion of the call starts, make sure that you're personable and energetic. The audio and video often tend to minimize your emotions instead of amplifying them. Don't get hysterical, but make sure there is no doubt that you're showing up at 110%. Stand up when you're recording if you can, as it opens up your lungs and helps with confidence. Make sure that you use the host's name and the show's name throughout the episode. Compliment the host and the show, and maybe even mention one of the previous episodes if you have a favorite. This should not be "great question" type of compliments, but a sincere compliment paid to the host. You can plan one or two of these before the interview, but this helps connect you with the host and they will be more likely to continue to share the episode and introduce you or promote you to others. Not only does this build rapport with the host, but it also builds trust with the listeners. They see you as one of them, a colleague.

When you're recording the interview, remember facts tell but stories sell. The typical podcast listener will remember your stories and forget most of the rest. If you want to record a truly memorable interview, focus on your stories.

If the interview includes prescripted questions, keep your answers short, to the point, and consistent with your goals. Avoid the tendency to reframe the question so that it fits into a particular narrative you want to talk about. The audience will not feel the value in that type of answer. In fact, listeners to shows with prescripted questions know the questions very well and listen because answers to those questions add value to them. Be sure to answer them, and to answer them in a way that leads to listeners wanting more information.

As you answer the questions and tell your stories, you will want to encourage listeners to go to your website for additional information. We call this an "offer" in this system. The offer is the key to achieving your goal of getting listeners to your website, where you can encourage them to engage more with you.

You need an offer for each podcast you're on. It can be the same offer, as for the most part, your podcast guest campaign is designed to put you in front of the same people (your ideal customers), so their needs and wants will generally be the same and you don't necessarily need multiple offers to entice them to visit you. If you're like me and have a few focuses within your expertise, which call for multiple pitch sheets, you may consider having the same amount of offers, with each tailored to the respective pitch sheet.

Typically more than one offer can give the listeners more chance to say "yes." Our testing has shown that giving three offers provides the listener to say yes to something a visit your site. Think of the three offers based on their level of excitement: yes, Yes, YES!

What is an offer?

An offer is something uniquely valuable to the listener that will encourage them to take action and visit your website. Examples of offers that require a minimum level of commitment (the little "yes") might include visiting your site to see a picture you talked about, watch a short video you referenced, or view a helpful infographic that you said would more fully answer a question. Often, the little "yes" isn't even placed behind a sign up page. In marketing terms it isn't designed to be "bait" to get a lead (which usually comes in the form of an email sign up) but a visit "bait" to get them to your website to look around and learn more.

Offers that require the larger Yes—a larger commitment—might include personal assessments, downloads, recorded training, or other documents you would typically send them through email. Because most people expect to get this type of information through email, it seems natural for them to provide at least some basic information like their name and email address.

A smaller percentage of listeners will likely hear you and respond with a very big YES! These are the ideal prospects who are ready to engage with you right away after hearing about you and your story on the podcast interview. They will likely view and download everything. They will spend time looking around your website to get to know you further. For them you will want to offer them an easy way to begin to work with you. Examples of these big YES offers could be a free consultation, a personal evaluation, or even to be part of a live webinar.

What the offer isn't.

The offer isn't a sell. Never, ever *sell* on a podcast. Your podcast interview is often the first "jab," the first "serve" in your relationship with the listeners. You still need to jab, or serve, at least two more times before you can effectively ask for something in return. Moreover, selling can make for an awkward discussion with the host, as the conversation can turn to a discussion on product specifications, price, and other things that take time away from you making a connection with the listeners.

It's perfectly fine to *talk about* products or services that you offer, but it's unrealistic to think that after knowing of you for thirty minutes someone that most will want to jump straight to the final step, pull out their credit card, and send you money. While the fast transaction can be common in some interviews when the guest is talking about a book, promoting a kickstarter campaign or offering an entry level product or service, it isn't the ultimate measure of success. The focus should not be on the initial sale but the lifetime value of the client. It's never been easier to make a transaction online (i.e. sell something once), but harder to build a profitable long-term relationship (i.e. build a brand or business) Focus on how you can nurture the relationship better, lead them from a listener (jab/serve), to a visitor (jab/serve), to a lead (jab/serve), and only then give them a reason to take the next step and buy your products or services (right hook/ask).

It's perfectly fine to discuss solutions to common problems that you provide, but offering products, especially with prices, is taboo. It's rude and tacky. It degrades the interview to an infomercial. Worse yet, because these podcasts will be heard for years—they are evergreen, there for downloading as long as the show is live—it can cause confusion among listeners down the road if you change your structure, prices, or focus because a new listener may connect with your interview months or years after it first airs and their first impression of you when they get to your site would not be favorable if you promised one thing on the show and they see another on the site.

Thus, the most effective—and evergreen—way to turn listeners into leads is to make an offer. Offers focus on adding unique value to the listener so if someone is interested in what you're saying, you're providing a place that they can go to gain more information. Your offer is your second "jab" or "serve" in your relationship with the listeners, after the content you give on the podcast. Offers must add unique value to your ideal customers. Encouraging them to visit the site to sign up to win a free iPad or gift card will likely get you more visitors and leads, but very few customers.

Mention your offer (or offers) multiple times during your interview, as repetition is the key to remembering. In addition, a compelling offer made in a personable way towards the beginning of the interview will have the listener thinking of you as a giver from the beginning and can enhance their acceptance of your expertise.

Making listeners wait until the end for the offer assumes that they will all listen until the very end, will have a pen and paper ready right then, or can remember a web address that is given only once. While that may be true for some of the listeners, some listeners perceive offers only made at the end as an upsell or sales pitch and will not receive them as well. Others learn the rhythm of a show and stop listening as the interview is wrapping up. Make it easier for the listeners to receive your offer well by mentioning it during the interview as a natural part of the conversation and repeating it a few times.

Because this section is about how to conduct the perfect interview, I will not spend too much time on what would create a compelling offer, which I will discuss in detail in the next section, however, the goal of an offer is to give the listeners a reason to go to your website, to take a small next step to continue a relationship with you.

A great example of using a unique offer to connect with listeners comes from a quilt maker. Because most podcasts are audio-only, you might think that it would be difficult for a quilt company to use a podcast guest campaign to get leads. But visual products can often work better on podcasts to move your ideal customers from being listeners to visitors. When talking about quilts on a sports podcast, talking about a quilt made for Wayne Gretzky and inviting listeners to see it by provide a memorable URL for the Welcome Page (more on this later) to visit can be very effective. It can also be very effective when promoting the quilts on a podcast to have mothers talk about cutting up children's clothing to make the most adorable quilts and encouraging people to visit your website to see examples of how they can reuse their children's clothing too.

As the interview wraps up, the host will likely ask you how people can get in touch with you. To maximize the effectiveness of your close, it's critical that you keep it simple. Don't give them too many options because they won't remember any of them. Instead, remind them of the valuable offers you mentioned during the conversation. Then remind them of the one place on your website they to go to see it all. This welcome page address should be short and easy to remember, like YourWebsite.com/ PodcastName. Repeat this address at least two times and remind them that it will be in the show notes. It may sound like "The best place is right on PodcastGuestProfits.com/PodcastName. There, the listeners of (podcast name) can find everything (host's first name) and I just talked about. Just go to PodcastGuestProfits.com/PodcastName to find all my contact information right along with more information about how to turn listeners into leads and podcasts into profits right at PodcastGuestProfits.com/PodcastName."

Immediately after the interview.

After the interview, the host may tell you that they've stopped the recording. This will be followed by some small talk, some back and forth. At this time, you'll want to thank the host and ask when the episode will air. Reassure them that you will be promoting this episode on your social media. This is also a great time to ask the host what you can do to serve them more. Do they need more guests? Could they use an introduction?

By making this offer, they will often respond and ask you if there's anything they can do for you. This is a prime time to show your interest in being on other podcasts and asking them for referrals or introductions to other podcasts where you might be a great guest. You will just have completed a great interview and jabbed/served several times already from pre-interview in building a relationship with them. You have built a relationship commenting on their posts, sharing their content, reviewing their podcast, and making it easy to have you on their show, and during the podcast by providing massive value to their audience. This is the perfect time to ask.

Once you're off the interview with them, head right to social media and drop them a tweet or a Facebook message saying how excited you were with them. You could also tweet out another message about your interview and how excited you are for it to air on the date the host just told you.

Finally, add additional value for the host to stand out from the rest of the interviews so that your show is one the host will want to promote or put on a top-episodes list. Immediately write a handwritten note or send a gift based on something you gather from them on the interview. Think outside the box. When Nick Pavlidis was on *Entrepreneur on Fire,* he learned that John Lee Dumas, who he knew was from Maine, missed eating Maine lobsters after moving to San Diego. Nick immediately sent two giant "thank you lobsters" straight from Maine to John. A few days later, John posted a video thanking Nick for the thoughtful gift. The smile on John's face was priceless and Nick stood out for the unique, thoughtful gift.

Often, it's not what was said in the interview but the relationship that was built that makes the difference between a one-off relationship with a podcaster and a long-term relationship that can lead to future business. Do something to show your generosity and thankfulness for this great opportunity to go from obscure to acclaimed by talking to their audience.

Remember, although you have just invested thirty minutes into this interview, the host will be spending hours more editing and promoting it. That exposure could have cost you thousands or tens of thousands of dollars if it was done over commercial radio or TV. Make sure to treat them well if you want to get invited back on their show and to be a great podcast guest. Show them how much you appreciate the value they provided you.

Action Steps:

1. Make a list of ten offers your ideal customer might value enough to exchange their contact information with you.

2. Narrow that list of ten offers down to the three you think are the highest value.

3. Create the first iteration of those top three offers. It doesn't need to be fancy. You can improve the looks over time. But even a bullet list of eight steps to drafting the perfect pitch sheet that you print to PDF from Microsoft Word would do just fine, assuming your ideal customer could benefit from knowing how to draft a perfect pitch sheet.

section two

BUILDING THE FUNNEL

TURNING LISTENERS INTO LEADS

Everything we've talked to up to this point is just the fuel for our marketing machine. Content is the fuel that drives our online marketing machine. Fuel without a machine doesn't provide results. A machine without fuel is just as useless. You might be surprised to know that the perfect interview is part of the fuel and not part of the funnel in my system. That is in no way to diminish the importance of the interview, as the interview is critical to getting listeners into our funnel. But the interview, without a well-oiled machine on the back-end, won't make any long-lasting results. The fuel, without a machine won't accelerate your business or take you from obscure to acclaimed. The funnel will.

The key to an effective funnel is that it's an automated *marketing* machine, not a *sales* machine. Some people refer to similar setups as a "sales funnel," but I hate and reject that term because it treats people as objects to be put and forced through a sales process, when a proper *marketing* machine is based upon nurturing leads to help them solve their problem with your product or service.

Without the marketing element based on helping people solve their problem, you end up treating individuals as numbers. They feel less valued. You both lose. They lose an opportunity to connect with you for information, products, and services that can help them in an area that is important to them. You lose an opportunity to grow your business and build relationships with your ideal customers. Remember, the goal isn't a quick conversion (sales) but building strong relationships that yield more profitable customers. Long-term profitable companies focus on retention and lifetime value or every customer. It's, thus, critical that any post-interview funnel focus on marketing, not just sales.

Our object isn't to *sell* anybody a product or service. It's to help them solve their problem or pain area, hopefully with a single or series of products or services we offer. Zig Ziglar said it clearly: You can get everything you want in life, if you help enough other people get what they want. Give them enough value and they will give you plenty of value in return.

At the end of the day, it doesn't matter how sophisticated your product or service is, we all sell Preparation-H. No matter what your product or service is, think of it as hemorrhoid cream. No one is excited about your product or service, they're excited about the relief it will provide them. You don't sell products or services. You sell the results they will provide. You can't provide relief with a "sales funnel." But you can with a marketing machine that provides real value and understanding. At the end of a podcast interview you should be seen as a valued partner, not a peddler. You marketing machine will deliver on this promise.

I will walk you through exactly how to do that in this section. As you might imagine, in order to do that, the first thing I recommend is to start building your online presence.

Your online presence

It doesn't matter what industry you're in or what you sell, you need an online presence. Everyone has an online presence. It can be used to build or destroy trust. It can be used to masterfully to turn listeners into leads. It must be clear, but it doesn't have to be complicated. Your online presence can be as simple as your social media profiles and a free web page to capture email addresses, or as complicated as a robust website that costs you thousands of dollars. For the purpose of using my system to turn listeners into leads, several free or low-cost options will do just fine as you start out and can be up and running in less than an hour.

The important thing to remember is that it's the strategy, not the tools, that makes this system work. What you *do* with the tools is much more important than what tools you use. Several years ago Dan Miller had a tree that had been struck by lightning and split in half. Instead of removing the rest of the tree, my friend called an artist who came by with a chainsaw and carved a beautiful eagle out of what was left of the tree. It's gorgeous. With a similar chainsaw, I nearly cut off my leg last winter cutting firewood. I was using the same tool as the artist, but the skill and creativity of the user resulted in two very different results. In this chapter, I'm going to show you the strategy, so that you acquire the skill and creativity to set up an effective online marketing funnel no matter what tools you choose to use.

Once you learn the system, get started. You can always improve over time as you learn. You can upgrade to more powerful and costly tools. The tools merely multiply and amplify the effect of your strategy, knowledge, and creativity. Start with a basic tool and you'll know when you need to move up to a more powerful, more expensive one in order to serve your customers even better. If you struggle with this you can also consider outsourcing it to someone who can set up the technical side and either operate the backend or train you to do so. I've done this for several clients and have seen others barter with others for setup services as well. For several recommendations of solutions in different price ranges, head on over to the resources page at www.PodcastGuestProfits.com/Resources.

You need an offer that is highly valuable to your ideal customer, and only your ideal customer.

As I mentioned in the secrets of the perfect interview section, delivering a compelling offer during your podcast interview can be a catalyst for developing long-term relationships with ideal customers. To maximize the effectiveness of your offer, however, the offer needs to be narrowly tailored to your ideal audience. Doing so provides several tangible and intangible benefits.

Think of your offer as a way to give your ideal customer —and only your ideal customer—a reason to go to your website. Just like our discussion about speaking to the *right* people and not just *a lot of* people, an effective offer will only be attractive to the *right* people. And just like many beginner podcast guests make the mistake of confusing volume with quality, many beginner online marketers make the mistake of confusing monetary value with practical value when creating offers. This is a big mistake that can cost you significant time and money.

Some ineffective offers include high-value giveaways that anyone and everyone would want, like an Amazon gift card or iPad. Although these items have high monetary value, they're attractive to everyone and tell you nothing about the people who visit your site to claim their chance. In fact, you may end up collecting 10,000 email addresses (which you will have to pay a monthly fee to manage) and find that only a few of those email addresses belong to potential customers.

To the contrary, an offer that
you would potentially work
focused list of potential cust
offers, include:

1. "Go to this website for a
   quiz) to see where you
   want to work on." Aaro
   uses a self-assessment very
2. "Go to this website for a checklist [or a tip sheet]." I offer six secrets to getting booked on podcasts. It's a very useful and targeted tip sheet because it's directly connected to my ideal customer's needs and wants and also lets them know that I have the knowledge to coach them or help them plan and run their *Podcast Guest Profits* campaign with them if they want even more from me.
3. If you're an author, you could offer a free workbook or first chapter of your book.
4. If you're in finance, you could offer an online tool or calculator to help listeners manage their money better.

As you can see, your offer doesn't need to be big or complex. It just needs to add value to your ideal customer and, ideally, nobody else.

You need a welcome page to deliver your offer and turn listeners into visitors.

Once you have your offer down, you will need a way to make your ideal listener feel at home that can turn listeners into visitors. If you have an existing website, this can be an additional page—a welcome page—that is he particular podcast to let the listeners re in the right place.

worry, you don't need to be a web developer to set up. I have set these up hundreds of times for clients nd myself and several of my clients do it themselves as well. If you want to see a video of me creating a landing page that can be duplicated and customized in less than ten minutes, along with a list of tools to use to do so, head over to the resources page. As with anything online, the tools aren't as important as the functionality and a WordPress webpage is just fine starting out as long as it performs the right steps.

Although it doesn't need to be fancy, the most effective welcome pages show the listeners that the page was built just for them right when they get there. Consider it a custom welcome page that will always be there ready to greet the listener if they visit the day the podcast airs or years later.

Remember, in the interview section you learned that when you're on a show, mention that you built a page just for listeners of that show where they can get your offer. This page is a continuation of the promise you made on the interview. It should build trust with the listener, who, if they see the welcome page, is now a visitor.

Building trust is key to getting visitors to take action. Testing done on ecommerce sites, blogs, and in the Podcast Guest Profit system has shown the importance of including trust seals. In ecommerce, this could be a Better Business Agency Seal. For a blog is could be a recognition or award. For you as a podcast guest, the ultimate trust seal is the podcast's name, artwork, and a picture of the host.

The listeners know, like, trust, and recognize the podcast and host. You, on the other hand, are relatively unknown. While they have heard you, they most likely will have no idea what you or your company look like. Make sure to greet them by name on the Welcome Page with a friendly brand they recognize, and a friendly image. This should be the podcast artwork and the host.

As you get more comfortable setting up the pages, or if you outsource this function, using elements like the podcast's colors and having a video or text welcome message that references the podcast name can enhance the user's experience by creating an additional sense of familiarity and comfort.

To further enhance user experience and help people connect with you, it's important to also keep the web address simple and familiar, with the most effective addresses being your site followed by the podcast or host's name or nickname, which listeners will have an easier time remembering. For example www.PodcastGuestProfits.com/FireNation would be a good option if I were to go back on *Entrepreneur on Fire,* as Fire Nation is what the host calls his listeners and they are already accustomed to using this for discount codes.

The perfect welcome page will build trust and authority and introduce yourself even more to the listener who's now become the visitor. Most hosts will appreciate that you're creating a unique page for their visitors and gladly let you use a couple of images off of their site. Beyond that, an effective welcome page will include a video or text message from you to welcome them, remind them what you and the host talked about, and direct them to the offer or offers you promised on the podcast.

Once you have this set up, you will have created the structure that allows you to turn listeners into visitors. The next steps will help you turn those visitors into leads.

Using the welcome page to convert visitors into leads.

Up to this point we have identified, connected with, and been interviewed on podcasts that reach our ideal customers. We have designed an irresistible offer or offers that will add value to our ideal customers by solving a problem they know they have. And we will have designed a welcome page to turn those listeners into visitors. This next step will help turn those visitors into leads to nurture into customers. What's the difference between a visitor and a lead? A lead is someone who's exchanged their contact information for one or more of your offers. They have made the first transaction with you, trading something of value they have (their contact information) for something of value they want from you (your offer). While no money has been exchanged this truly is the first micro-sale that further builds trust and leads to a more profitable relationship.

As with most of this system, this setup can be done very simply on your own and doesn't need to cost any money to be effective. One very basic way to set this up is with a sign-up form that you can get from an email service provider. Email service providers can range from free basic services like Mailchimp, to high-cost service providers like HubSpot or InfusionSoft. The decision about which tool to use can depend on the number of e-mail addresses you manage (your list), how many e-mails you send, and the depth of analytics and automation you desire. I include references to several service providers on the resources page, but to keep it simple for the purpose of this book, a free service should work just fine.

Making
provider
No matte
thumb is
Keep it Si
minimum
this will i
so you ca
mails. In s
you may v
about the
talked abo
customers
enter their
Walker fro
early on. If
for a zip co ... you if you can
even help them with an open territory. These qualifying questions can help you further identify your perfect customer. They let you manage your time and provide the most value to the lead. Sometimes the answer will let you know when a particular lead would be better served by offering to refer them to someone who could better serve them.

Once the lead has entered their information, your job becomes nurturing your relationship with them. The first step to do so is to promptly deliver the on your promise. Deliver the offer or offers that you promised and they requested. There are several ways to do so, no matter what e-mail service provider you use. If yours doesn't include file delivery, here are two free ways to do so. First, you could upload the offers to an unlisted page on your website and include a link to that page on your e-mail confirmation. This can be okay starting out, but can also have your offer be visible to the public, so if you go this route, you should consider adding a password to that

ou will e-mail them the
ir information, and then
our confirmation e-mail as
vould be to put the offer or offers
r other file-sharing service and then
the folder in the confirmation e-mail.

have followed through on your promise to
lue to them, first during the interview (which
you turn a listener into a visitor) and then by
ng a welcome page and form to exchange contact
nformation for the offer or offers you promised on the interview (which helped you turn the visitor into a lead), you must continue to serve if you want to turn that lead into a customer. Remember, it can take seven or more contacts before enough trust is made to turn that lead into a customer.

Although the specifics of how to turn a lead into a customer will vary greatly depending on your specific product or service, your ideal customer's wants and needs, the price point of your products or services, and much, much more. It's important that you remain in regular contact with your leads and provide additional value on a regular basis. I have included several examples of nurturing sequences that my clients and I have used on the resources page so you can get some ideas, but by this point you will know your business and ideal customer enough that the important lesson is to keep moving. There are no magic words to turn leads into customers. Warning: Copying an email that worked for another business to another group may actual destroy trust. I've seen far too many people copy or use swipe files. The tone is never consistent. Use your own words. Remember they got this far because they connected with what you said.

One next step might be to schedule webinars to talk further about the issues and e-mailing your list to let them know. Another might be to ask them a question that shows them you care and helps you design more offers, products, or services to help solve those problems, such as asking them to tell you something they're struggling with right now. Another next step might be to e-mail them a couple of weeks out to ask them if they had a chance to review the offer or offers and if they have any questions. Yet another great next step might be to offer to spend ten minutes with them on the phone to get to know them better and help them start to solve their problems.

The important thing is to follow up with them in a way that encourages them to move forward to solving their problem or pain point. You want them to take additional action to improve whatever situation caused them to go from listener to visitor to lead in the first place. The more you can help them improve their situation, the more they will trust you and associate you with that improvement, and the closer they will come to becoming a customer.

PROMOTION: FUELING YOUR MARKETING MACHINE

If a tree falls in the forest and no one is there to hear it, does it make a noise? You can debate the science behind that question all you want, but whether it makes a noise or not, if no one is there to hear it, does it really matter?

If your podcast interview goes live and no one listens to it, does it make a noise? Similar to the tree falling in a forest question, the technical answer doesn't matter. If nobody listens to it, that means nobody goes from listener to visitor to lead to customer. No one gets value from the time you invested researching that podcast, preparing for the interview, creating the offer or offers, setting up the welcome page, or adding the proper e-mail collection form.

You can have the best setup in the world, and if you do, your odds of success will be increased. No matter how great your message and machine are, the key to adding the most value to the listeners, the host, and you, is for you and the host is to ensure the maximum number of people know about the interview. You need to promote the episode. In fact, once you have the infrastructure in place, the number one thing you can do to supercharge your marketing machine for the long term is to actively promote each of your episodes.

Too many guests wrongly assume that promotion is the responsibility of the podcaster. Part of the reason podcasters have guests on is to cross-pollinate audiences. They want access to your audience, even if it's more limited than theirs, just as you want access to their audience. In nature, Cross-pollination bears fruit. The same is true in podcasts. The podcaster will invest significant time and money promoting your episode with show notes on their site, on social media, and by posting it to podcast delivery apps like Stitcher and iTunes. Your additions to this will help build momentum and encourage the podcaster to want you back, refer you to other podcasters, recommend you to listeners, and even engage with you as a customer.

How to promote your podcast episode.

The primary methods for episode promotion include online platforms like websites or blogs, e-mail distribution, and social media platforms. Just think of anywhere your ideal customers could already be. Each of these methods typically has free and paid options. The free methods should add plenty of fuel to your marketing machine. The paid options should be the exception for testing and promoting key interviews. In this section, I'll describe the highest-impact free methods in each category along with one or two paid options to consider when the time is right. Paying for promotion might make sense when you want to reach a specific group of people with a high-value offer that you have struggled to reach with free promotion, for example.

If you have a blog or website, write a new post or a media/appearances page that promotes your interview. This is a great, free way to use your existing online presence to promote the show to visitors, leads, and customers, reinforcing you as an expert in the industry. You can also ask the podcaster if you can add the podcast episode to your own site, which is also called "embedding" the episode on your site. Make your own show notes that link back to the podcast host's website.

Never just copy the show notes the host has created. The search engines despise duplicate content and can often punish you by making you show up lower in searches.

Make sure to check with the host to get permission first before adding or embedding the episode on your site. Podcasts are copyrighted materials. While I've never heard of anyone getting sued for such copyright infringement, it's possible, and as a guest it's just plain unprofessional and rude not ask first. Most podcasters will be very happy and even honored for you to do so. Pat Flynn, for example, who was the top podcaster in 2015 and is host of the Smart Passive Income podcast has said he doesn't care where people hear his show, just so long as they hear it.

There are countless ways to pay to promote on blogs or other websites. For example, you could pay to advertise your episode in search engines with paid services like Google Adwords, although that isn't something I would necessarily recommend to the typical person. Purchasing space on other relevant blogs, or even paying the podcaster for advertising space that keeps your episode prominently featured, however, could be well worth your while, as it puts your episode front and center for new listeners to discover, who you already know are highly likely to be ideal prospective customers.

If you have an e-mail list, definitely email your list to let them know about your interview, linking to the show notes, as well as to the podcaster's feed in iTunes and Stitcher. This will help your existing leads and customers get more value from you with only one click. It's a simple way to make it easy for them to hear your voice, get additional value from you, and continue nurturing leads and existing customers. Adding a section on recent media interviews to your emails can show remind readers that you're an in-demand expert in your area. For a tutorial on how to link directly to an iTunes or Stitcher feed, head on over to the resources page.

Although it isn't as common as website advertising, some content providers will allow you to pay to promote to their e-mail list provided the content will add value to their subscribers. This can be a good way to reach new audiences through a trusted referral if the list matches your goals.

Finally, with social media. As with e-mail and other online promotion tools, there are several free and paid ways to gain attention through social media. Free methods include promoting on personal or professional Facebook pages, in Facebook groups, on individual or collaborative Pinterest boards, on Twitter, in personal or group LinkedIn feeds, through an Instagram account that is linked to your media page, and more. Be sure to share your content on all relevant channels, and several times, at different times of the day and over several days. With so much content being posted, the lifespan of one social media post is very short, often just minutes. Thus, no matter how large an audience is, posting a link to your episode just one time will reach only a very small fraction of your free potential.

There are also several paid ways to promote through social media. Facebook, LinkedIn, Twitter, Instagram, and Pinterest all offer ways to very-effectively target audiences based on characteristics like we talked about when we were targeting podcasts. In Facebook, for example, you can include income, gender, specific employers, age, marital or parental status, location, and more. You can even target people who have "liked" the podcast's or one of your competitors' pages (or both), acts that tell you a person is likely to be interested in your materials. Because there are so many powerful paid options for social media advertising, extra care should be taken to make sure any money spent is done so with as much impact as possible targeted to your ideal potential customers.

What I have found works well with my clients is to schedule online promotion to begin immediately and continue for at least six months. We post at least two to three times the first day on Twitter, at least daily for the first week, and at least once every two weeks for the rest of the six months. We analyze the effectiveness of the tweets every ninety days to see which ones get the most engagement and adjust accordingly. Including relevant hashtags like #podcast and any that relate to your offer or industry on sites like Instagram, Twitter, and Facebook will help further your reach to include people who search those hashtags. Be sure to always include the host and the podcast accounts in your posts. We all listen for our own names. The host of the podcast is no different. When they see you promoting your interview it will continue to build a relationship with them. It will remind them of your interview and show them you're mentioning and promoting them often. You continue to serve and build trust. Although it sounds like a lot of work, several free or low cost programs exist that can help. Social Media Juke Box, Hootsuite, and Meet Edgar can help you with scheduling and analysis. Some empower you to schedule a post one time and have it shared over and over again. Because social media platforms and functionality are constantly sharing, it's especially important to check the latest tools and techniques for increasing efficiency and effectiveness. We will keep you up to date on the resources page, including the latest tips, techniques, and resources.

Optimizing the Promotions

With almost any of these methods, one-off promotion will provide a "snapshot" effect, offering a bump in attention for days or weeks, tops. Here are four ways to optimizing promotions so your marketing machine churns much longer.

1. Build a library for continuous sharing.

Continually sharing and building a library of appearances for your current and prospective ideal customers to see is not only acceptable, but wise. Podcasts, and especially well-executed podcast interviews like what you will deliver, are what we call evergreen content. This means they're available and remain relevant long into the future. This means that there are millions of people who will first discover your episode days, weeks, months, or even years after it goes live. Promoting it multiple times over a course of months or years is important to make sure your episode and offers reaches those latecomers. In fact, because your content adds value to their lives, you will be doing your ideal customers a disservice if you don't share your high-value, evergreen content over and over again.

2. Get visual.

You can also increase the impact of any of these methods by adding images and videos to your promotions. On social media, images and videos help you stand out in a crowded feed and encourage people to reshare to their followers. In e-mail, images help encourage people to take action by clicking. And when promoting on blogs and websites, images encourage people to read and then share posts and also get people's attention on traditional advertisements like buttons in the sidebar.

Some options for artwork could include the artwork that the host makes for your episode, which not only promotes your episode, but also the podcast in general. You could even have a scrolling banner on the homepage of your website that says "as seen on" with images of the shows acting as social proof of your expertise and relevance. Bigger celebrities often include national news outlets on their sites, but relevant, well-known podcasts can provide very effective instant proof for new hosts that may be considering you for their show or visitors who might otherwise only give your site a few seconds of attention.

3. Repurpose the Content.

Audio and video podcasts are incredible sources of multi-purpose content. Because many people prefer reading to listening, or listening to watching, or any other combination, having your content available in multiple formats will help you reach ideal customers no matter what their consumption preferences. For people who prefer shorter bites of information, you could make short video or audio clips to share. With a video interview, you can use free tools to separate the audio into a file people can download on their phone. Audio files can be transcribed to text. Text files can be broken down and edited further into multiple blog posts or even further for social media posts to direct people to the podcast and your offers. Finally, you could even take that transcript and use it as the basis for a longer-form project like a book.

Some hosts offer transcriptions of their episodes right from their site. Pat Flynn of the *Smart Passive Income* podcast and Jaime Masters, of *The Eventual Millionaire* podcast are two examples of shows that offer everyone a free transcription of all of their episodes. It's very easy to transcribe audience interviews. If you need to do it yourself, you can find people on rev.com or Fiverr to audio for one dollar per minute or less. Once you have that transcription you can then break out blog posts, tweets, or even short quotes to use on images and share as pearls of wisdom directly from you.

4. Collaborate and Exchange Mutual Support.

At the end of your interview, the host may ask you to record a quick clip promoting the podcast. It's usually something simple like "Hi, this is Tom Schwab from PodcastGuestProfits.com and you're listening to my favorite career podcast, *48 Days to the Work You Love* with Dan Miller." Recording that gives you an opportunity for additional exposure on the episode and I highly advise agreeing to do so.

Being asked also gives you a great opportunity to ask for a similar recorded testimonial in return to help you promote your business or episode. Something to the effect of "This is Dan Miller from *48 Days to the Work You Love.* Check out my friend, Tom Schwab, the only podcast guest campaign manager I recommend at PodcastGuestProfits.com." Or you could ask the host to record a short clip to promote the particular episode to help you enhance and add additional variety to your promotions. That type of clip would sound something like this: "This is Dan Miller from *48 Days to the Work You Love* and I encourage you to check out my interview with Tom Schwab where he shares six outstanding secrets to profiting as a podcast guest." Those short clips can help both of you promote the podcast and your larger brands. Be sure to look for openings to ask and ask in return if the host brings it up first.

TUNING YOUR ENGINE FOR EVEN MORE HORSEPOWER

If you have ever owned a car for more than a few months you know that regular upkeep and maintenance are key to improving your car's efficiency and life. Oil changes, tune-ups, and scheduled service help you get maximum power and effectiveness out of your car. The same is true with your online marketing machine. The first pitch sheet, welcome page, and promotional campaign can yield highly valuable information to help you constantly improve and achieve better and better results. It's very important that you assess your materials and methods at least every ninety days to see what's working and what isn't. Then refine your systems to get the maximum results from every interview.

Because of the way you set up your machine, the system will allow you to collect all sorts of data to analyze and adjust on each individual podcast interview. You may be able to get download numbers for some hosts, to see your episode's total reach. You can then see how many listeners visited your welcome page. You can see how many visitors became leads. Then you can examine how many lead became customers after you nurtured them. After several episodes you will also be able to start comparing numbers between episodes and identify averages to help plan in the future. You will be able to make informed decisions on what works and what doesn't.

There's an old joke in marketing that says that half of the time and money you spend on marketing will be wasted, but you never know what half it is. It's funny to marketers because it's so true and so painful. Because this system has been designed and refined with the help of over one hundred podcasters and over one thousand interviews, that joke will not apply to your marketing machine. The more you interview, the more you will be able to adjust and make your machine continually run easier, more efficiently, and more effectively, so that every interview you do gives you the results you want.

The system is designed to make sure you don't have to listen to me or other experts' opinions either. Sure, the system I am sharing with you is based on best practices refined over a long time and across industries. The system is powerful and proven, providing you with the best foundation for conduction a podcast guest campaign that converts. Ultimately, however, your listeners, visitors, leads, and customers will tell you what works best and where to tweak.

For example, if you speak to 1,000 people on a podcast, but only two visit your welcome page the listeners are telling you that you were either speaking to the wrong people, had sub-par audio, were not coming across as an expert, or were not offering a useful enough offer to turn the listeners into visitors (or a combination of those). If you're getting a high percentage of listeners visiting your site, but not many are opting in, it's telling you something about your welcome page. If you're getting a high percentage of opt-ins, but not a lot of engagement beyond that, then the issue is your nurturing. In other words, once the system is in place, listen much more to what the listeners and your customers are telling you through their actions than what some expert (including me) tells you about your system. Everyone has an opinion. The listeners, visitors, leads, and customers have your answers.

Growing up, I was told sometimes being smart is knowing the right answer when told. If you're smart enough to listen to your experts, they will tell you what they love and what they loathe. Listen to them. Listen to their actions and then take action yourself. Double down on what their actions tell you they love. Stop doing what they loathe.

If you tell a story on a podcast that results in a lot of visits and comments, keep that story in the repertoire. If you have a product that sells off the shelf, make and promote that product more often. Then design a next-step product to serve them even better. If you have a product that's a dud, consider tweaking or dropping it because they're telling you it's not something they need or value.

Consider sending a short survey by e-mail asking what they thought of the interview, offers, communication, or product. Doing so will let them know you how to serve better not just work harder.

By learning from your listeners, leads, and customers your marketing machine will continually get better and more efficient. You will serve the listeners, visitors, leads, and customers better. And when you do this, they will reward you handsomely with more and more certificates of appreciation, those green pieces of paper with pictures of dead Presidents.

I suggest doing a tune-up every ninety days. This allows you to gather enough behavioral data to do a meaningful assessment. Doing it more often will probably mean that you're looking at more noise than data. Don't make decisions based on anecdotes. Base them on actual hard evidence because "the plural of anecdote is not data," as

John Johnson reminds us in *EVERYDATA: The Misinformation Hidden in the Little Data You Consume Every Day*. Intentionally doing a review once a quarter allows you to step back, be more objective, and make wise decisions based on facts to move forward. Let's look at how to conduct a quarterly tune-up next.

Conducting a quarterly tune-up

The need for a quarterly tune-up can't be overstated. In fact, when first developing and refining the system one client and I were looking back at one year of podcast interviews, a year in which he was interviewed on over one hundred shows, to see where we could make improvements. Because he had used this system, he had increased visitors, leads, and customers. We were incredibly happy with the raw numbers.

We were surprised to discover, however, that ninety five percent of his visitors came from only thirty percent of his interviews. Although the natural reaction might be to consider the seventy percent of interviews the yielded only five percent of traffic as time wasted, quite the opposite is true. Each of those interviews told us something that could be improved in the future. Some shows were selected poorly. Some stories didn't sell. Some offers were not perceived as valuable. Without information about what did not work, he could never have been able to appreciate precisely what did. By using this system and setting up interview-specific welcome pages, we were able to get incredible insights that helped us adjust big in year two.

His next hundred interviews were even more successful than the first. He dropped the stories that flopped, offered the highest-converting offers, doubled down on products that were well received, and dropped what didn't work. His results became supercharged and yours can, too, by setting up a system that can collect data and then assessing that data on a regular basis.

Don't worry, I'm going break out all the relevant measures right here, all of which is available to you for free. Moreover, with only one exception, all of the information is under your control, with the only exception being episode downloads. Generally the only way to get that information is from the podcast host and not all hosts are willing to share that information. If you build a relationship with them and let them know that you're working to improve your systems and add value to more people they might just give you that information after ninety days if you promise to keep it confidential. The episode download number is useful to tell you the raw percentage of listeners who visited your welcome page.

Like I mentioned above, that percentage helps you assess and improve several parts of your campaign. If you can't get that data, don't worry, you can still improve and perfect that part of your campaign by asking your leads and customers what attracted you to them and assessing the other data that you will gather. Because the rest of the data is completely under your control, I'm going to spend the bulk of this section on where to get that data and what it tells you, starting first with analyzing your visitor data from your welcome page.

If you're using a WordPress site to host your welcome page, you can get view counts for free using tools like Google Analytics or the JetPack plugin. Those will also tell you how many pages each visitor looked at and how long they spent on your site. That tells you their level of engagement and whether you built trust and authority through your welcome page. If people are visiting multiple pages or spending a lot of time on your site, it's a positive sign that your welcome page positions you as a trustworthy authority. If they leave quickly, which is known as bouncing, you know you have done something wrong. You haven't quickly met their expectations.

The next thing to look at is the number of leads generated. Remember, leads are visitors who exchanged their contact information for your offer or offers. This tells you whether people wanted to make that first direct interaction with you and trusted you with their contact information. Look at which offers gave the best leads, which offers converted the best, and which calls to action resulted in people sharing their e-mail address with you.

Your basic quarterly assessment also needs to analyze how many customers you got that you could attribute to podcast interviews. Because you will be setting up a separate welcome page for each interview, you can even assess which podcasts performed best for you. Chances are the host also received great feedback about your episode. That may be a good opportunity to reach out to the podcast host to let them know that you have had great follow-up to the episode and would love to continue to serve their audience with an additional interview and new offer.

Finally, look at your e-mail manager to analyze your efforts to nurture the leads. Most e-mail providers will show you rich data that will help you better understand what your leads and customers think of your e-mail nurturing. The first relevant number is your "bounce rate." This tells you what percentage of your e-mails make it to their inbox. Sometimes people change email addresses when they change cable providers for example and don't update their e-mail address with you. When e-mails don't make it to an active inbox, that's called as a "bounce." If people make up fake emails just to get an offer, this can also be reflected in the "bounce rate"

You can also look at open and click rates. What percentage of your subscribers opened your e-mail? What percentage clicked on a link? Open rates are an expression of interest. If you're getting a high percentage, that tells you they're interested in you and the subject line seemed to indicate there was value in the e-mail. As you send more e-mails or grow your list larger, experiment with your subject lines to see how that translates into open rates. Testing different subject lines could drastically help your open rates and give you a better chance to have the content of your e-mails help earn their business.

Like open rates, click rates are also an expression of interest, however they also tell you quite a bit about how much your subscribers trust you. If people don't trust you, the only link they will be inclined to click is the unsubscribe link. If they really don't know, like, or trust you, they might just mark you as spam. If you put a link or a call to action in your e-mail, check what percentage of subscribers clicked on it. Adjust your calls to action and compare the click rates. You could check whether the raw web address like www.podcastguestprofits.com/resources works better than a URL embedded behind words, which are known as anchor text. Do more of what works and less of what doesn't.

The last piece of data, your unsubscribe rate, is challenging to look at objectively when first starting out. You have put so much time, thought, and effort into building incredible value for people and connected with them enough that they got enough value from you that they gave you their e-mail address to keep in touch and then one day they unsubscribe.

It's hard not to take that personally, I know, but I implore you to use all your objectivity to not take it personally. People unsubscribe for so many reasons, and sometimes no reason at all. Sometimes people do a complete subscription purge using an automated service like unroll.me. Other times people have stopped working in the niche that attracted them to you in the first place. Still other times someone might unsubscribe because they simply lose interest or focus on your topic, even if they still work in your industry. The point is that there are so many reasons that someone might unsubscribe and only one of them is you.

For purposes of tuning up your marketing machine, the general percentage of unsubscribes is helpful, along with any optional reasons they give during the automated unsubscribe process, is the most important factor. Among those reasons is that they lost interest, didn't mean to sign up, and, the kiss of death, that your emails were spam. If you're getting a lot of people reporting you as spam, that tells you that you're selling too much or too hard. You're asking, not serving. You aren't adding value. You may consider making your e-mails more conversational and increasing your serve, serve, serve, sell ratio in your e-mail nurturing because even a small percentage of spam reports can cause your e-mail to be flagged and not delivered. You want to make sure that people see you as an authoritative, helpful resource, and not a snake-oil salesperson.

Assessing your offers

In addition to the web and e-mail stats, your quarterly assessment needs to see what offers had the best engagement. We typically suggest having two or three different offers on every welcome page to see which one performs best. Remember we discussed giving listeners the opportunity to say yes, Yes, YES! Which one did best? Which one did worst?

Each quarter, on new interviews stop talking about the worst performing offer and replace it with a new one to test. Not only will this potentially help your conversion rate but it makes sure that you're always offering your visitors the most helpful, and fresh information.

Assess social stats and engagement.

Although not always as important as conversion rates, social stats are useful to provide social proof to get more interview opportunities and help you optimize your social media promotion to direct more people into your marketing machine.

Look at your social media stats including follower count, likes, shares, and other engagement. Many platforms like Pinterest, Twitter, Facebook, and even third-party apps like Buffer or Hootsuite can tell you which posts had the most engagement. Note which podcasts, posts, or pictures had the most clicks, shares, comments, and more. This tells you what people within your social reach liked best and what to do more of. Repost the best performing posts over and over again manually or through a service like Meet Edgar for people who didn't see it the first time or need to be reminded and use those posts as templates for other, future posts, looking at things such as the imagery, font size and style, title, subtitle, and timing,

Compile, adjust, and repeat.

Once you have analyzed the data, identify the relevant takeaways, adjust, and repeat. Which podcast performed the best? Which performed the worst? Which hosts got the best engagement? Was the root cause the host? Did they do a great job at promoting it, of asking the questions, of having the right audience? Or was it the audience? Could it be the different offers you made or the stories you told? Could it be the level of promotion by either the host or yourself? Look at the seasonality. Could it be the timing? Did a holiday help or hurt your results? Is one time of year better or worse than others?

If you still have questions, reach out to some of the hosts and ask your new leads and customers what they think. You might find that your ideal customers don't listen to a particular show that you thought would be a perfect fit. You might find that some hosts promoted more or better than others or some hosts had a personal crisis that caused them to pause all promotion efforts, leaving the visitor data from their show suspect. You might find that some shows get more traffic than expected, but lower engagement, while others get less traffic but higher engagement than expected.

Although this system is designed to put you in the best position to succeed and provide you trackable information to help you do so, you must analyze your results in order to improve your results over time. Do more of what worked well and less of what didn't work so well. Find shows that are similar to the ones that performed best and begin to serve and provide value to the hosts so you can begin to form a relationship with them. Reach out to the hosts of the best performing shows for the opportunity to be interviewed again, ask for referrals to similar podcasts, or discuss possible joint venture opportunities. Because you obviously brought value to their audience, and vice versa, a joint venture opportunity is a logical next step.

The wonderful thing about this system, and marketing machine you will build based on it, is that it's reproducible. You can treat it much like the directions on your shampoo: wash, rinse, and repeat. Every time you conduct a quarterly tune-up, you learn, adjust, and move forward. You will become more efficient, provide greater value, and get more out of each interview, as your marketing machine becomes better and better.

OVERDRIVE: OUTSOURCING EVERYTHING EXCEPT THE INTERVIEW

Up to this point, we've talked about how you can grow your business through fueling and building a podcast guest marketing machine. In this chapter, I will show you how to shift your machine into overdrive by outsourcing everything but the interview. Once your machine is fully operational, you will quickly find that the best use for your time will be interviewing on the right podcasts as much as possible and overseeing the quarterly tune-ups.

You will quickly find this chapter to be your favorite. This chapter will help you scale. This chapter will allow you to do even more than you've ever dreamed of. This chapter will help free you to do what you do best and outsource the rest who can do the other items better and cheaper than you. The whole idea of presenting yourself as an expert podcast guest is that you're the talent. You're a performer. You're the rock star, the headliner. You're the Rolling Stones or Taylor Swift.

When is the last time you saw the Rolling Stones setting up their instruments? When is the last time you saw Taylor Swift doing a microphone check? The answer is never. The performers perform because that is where their time is best spent. They perform and they work on their craft. That's it. They outsource everything else. They don't do the promotion. They aren't the roadies. And they don't drive the bus. To maximize the impact of their time and be as effective as possible, they outsource everything except for what they do best and what they have to do.

"Sinatra only sang," as one of our Interview Valet clients put it. This wise businessman understood the power of leverage. He wanted to be the guest and have others to the rest. You're no different than Sinatra, The Rolling Stones, or Taylor Swift in this way. You're just most likely in a different industry. Like them, your time is best spent doing what you do best and outsourcing the rest to people who can do those tasks better and cheaper than you. Like them, outsourcing will allow you to improve your skills—in this case interviewing and serving customers—because it will free up your time to do more of that. Like them, you will get better results with less effort by outsourcing. It will also be more fun for you.

I realize that when first starting out, budgets may feel tight and your first inclination may be to save money by doing everything yourself, but I strongly encourage you against attempting to do so. Although many back-end tasks are easy and repetitive, they eat up a lot of valuable time and every minute you're working on something other than speaking to and serving customers, you're limiting your reach and costing yourself money in the long run. In fact, if you took a list of my Podcast Guest Profits clients and ranked them by how successful they have been since starting the program, you would find a direct relationship between outsourcing and results. Our best performing clients outsourced the most because outsourcing the back-end allows you to be on multiple podcasts every week, or day, while still running your business.

Once you become open to outsourcing, the first question is naturally what to outsource. Although the ultimate goal for maximum impact is to outsource everything but the interview, when starting out, the answer to the question may vary depending on your skills, interests, and experience.

The best things to outsource first are the tasks that you don't like to do. If you love creating webpages but hate scheduling social media posts, you will be much more productive and successful if you outsource the social media part of your marketing machine. Outsourcing the tasks you don't like to do will help you get more done and stay motivated because you will enjoy what you're doing.

Once you outsource everything that you don't like to do, the next things to outsource are tasks that you aren't excellent at. Most of us can learn things. Most of us can get good at things, but if you aren't truly excellent at a task, it's best to get someone else to do it who is. If you're good, but not excellent at designing the offers that your leads will downloads in exchange for their contact information, stick to the substance and let someone else handle the design.

Finally, once you have outsourced everything you don't like to do and everything you enjoy but aren't excellent at doing, start outsourcing tasks that don't maximize the value and impact of your time. You may enjoy and excellent at computer programming, but programming your own website instead of talking to and serving customers will not grow your business.

Once you've decided what tasks you will outsource, the second question becomes to whom do you outsource. It's important that you outsource them to the right people and appreciate that there is no Wonder Woman or Superman who can do all of the tasks with excellence. While hiring one, generalist assistant is helpful for day-to-day operational tasks, you should not expect them to be able to do everything you need for your podcast guest campaign well. Remember, the goal is to maximize the impact of your resources. Because of that, the goal for outsourcing should be to put a small, but excellent team

.. of between three and five people who collectively possess the following five basic skills:

1. **Scheduling/Booking.** This person is like your concert promoter. They research podcasts to identify the right podcast for you to pitch, pitches you to them, coordinates schedules, confirms appointments in your calendar, and sends you all information needed for the interview.

2. **Social media management.** Someone on your team needs to take your episodes and promotes them on social media on an ongoing basis. They should understand which platforms would work best for your niche and how to optimize images, hashtags, and messages across platforms, as well as how to increase the efficiency and reach of your postings

3. **Webpage building.** The hardest web work will be building and optimizing your welcome page. Once that is in place, you will have a template that can be copied and tweaked for each interview. Although the duplication and tweaking exercises can be very repetitive and easy tasks, it's advisable to work with someone who designs webpages with excellence and works with others as well, as they will be able to help you constantly improve your welcome pages based on the performance of your pages and others.

4. **Funnel management.** You'll need someone to set up your nurturing and marketing funnels, including setting up systems for delivering your offers, collecting your leads, managing your e-mail campaigns, and designing your calls to action. Your funnels will typically need to be set up once, evaluated during your quarterly tune-up, and adjusted as needed. For this position, it's important to engage someone with digital marketing experience,

inbound marketing experience, and access to a good graphic designer, because they will be able to understand the process, content, and design to maximize the impact of your funnels.

5. **Audit and statistics analysis.** You'll need someone who understands relevant metrics and can advise you and your team on adjusting and improving based upon the results of your quarterly audit. This might be the hardest skill to hire, but it's vital to constant and meaningful improvement.

Now that you know what you will outsource and what skills you need to have on your team, the next question becomes where to find people who possess those skills. If you already have a team, some of your answers may be found within to your organization already. If not, or if you don't have people within your organization with the skills and capacity to take on additional projects, I suggest hiring outside help on an as-needed basis in the form of individual freelancers or agencies.

The benefits of hiring outside help on an as-needed basis include that you will often be working with specialists who work on and learn from many projects and keep up with the latest tools and techniques, you likely won't have to buy or maintain software or equipment because they will have it already, and your costs will typically be less compared to hiring someone on a full-time basis. The downsides include that you will have less oversight on day-to-day activities, might experience higher turnover, and might have to kiss a few frogs before you find your prince.

Here are three places to find people outside of your organization to add to your team:

1. **Referrals.** This is—by far—the best place to find people. Getting a referral from someone who has worked with a freelancer or agency helps cut down on the frog to prince ratio.

2. **Online boards.** This can be bit hit or miss, but sites like Fiverr, Upwork, Inbound.org, or Craigslist is full of freelancers advertising their services. Many of the sites also allow you to post a project with a budget and have freelancers reach out to you. To maximize your likely frog to prince ratio, be sure to look at reviews and previous work and interview a few freelancers. When you're just starting out, I also suggest giving a few of the same small jobs to three or four freelancers to see who best fits your needs and personality. Although giving the same assignment to multiple freelancers may increase your costs up front, it's one of the few ways to be able to compare what it would be like to work with each of them.

3. **Agencies.** Agencies can be more expensive than hiring a few freelancers, but have the ability to provide a true done-for-you solution. Although agencies do vary in the quality and breadth of their work, they have their own brand reputations to protect, and are thus often careful to provide top-quality work. There are different types of agencies, from full-service public relations agencies to specialist agencies. A full-service public relations agency may worthwhile, although it can be very expensive with a high monthly retainer. You could also find specialist agencies that just focus on a certain task, like social media management, and hire the rest of your team through freelancing sites or referrals.

With any of these options, it's important that your team appreciates the big picture of what they're helping you accomplish. For example, when we help our clients with their podcast guest campaigns, we provide everything but the interviews. Our company, Interview Valet, has a complete agency with team members who help with web design, social media, inbound strategy, buyer funnels, podcast outreach and relations, graphic design, statistics and oversight. We provide full, white-glove service so that our clients can concentrate on the interviews.

What makes our agency so valuable to our clients is that our team members understand the marketing machine and the role they play in the bigger picture. If you're building a team of internal candidates, freelancers, or agencies, it's important that your team members have a similar understanding so they work together to achieve your overall goals.

section three

YOUR 30-DAY PLAN FOR PODCAST GUEST PROFITS

GETTING STARTED FAST

Congratulations! You now have all the knowledge you need to profit as a podcast guest. You know how to decide who you want to speak with, where to find them, and how to connect with them. You know how to build a marketing machine to collect leads and nurture them into customers. Finally, you know how to take that marketing machine into overdrive by outsourcing everything but the interview. That's the good news. That's the opportunity.

The challenge, however, is none of that knowledge will help you until you take action. That's what this section is all about, helping you take action so that your marketing machine is up and running by this time next month.

DAY	ACTIVITY
1	Identify the Demographic and Psychographic attributes of your Ideal Customers
2	List at least fifty podcasts in a spreadsheet that could be potential fits using the exercises at the end of Chapter __.
3	Screen the podcasts you identified on Day 2 using the exercises at the end of Chapter __. Move any that don't pass to a different list to identify them as having been analyzed already.

DAY	ACTIVITY
4	Add columns to your spreadsheet for blogs, and social media handles for the shows or hosts that made the cut. Begin sharing content from at least five of those podcasts and commenting on blogs.
5	Comment on at least three blogs from your list of podcasts. Retweet or otherwise share social posts of at least five podcast hosts from shows that have passed your screening. Review one of the podcasts on iTunes. Share a screenshot of your review on social media, tagging the show and/or host.
6	Reach out to at least three people who are relevant to your industry and niche and ask if they will give you a testimonial. Comment on at least three blogs from your list of podcasts. Retweet or otherwise share social posts of at least five podcast hosts from shows that have passed your screening. Review one of the podcasts on iTunes. Share a screenshot of your review on social media, tagging the show and/or host.

DAY	ACTIVITY
7	If you don't have a logo, get one created. If you need help finding an affordable place to get a quality logo, head over to the resources page for several suggestions. Comment on at least three blogs from your list of podcasts. Retweet or otherwise share social posts of at least five podcast hosts from shows that have passed your screening. Review one of the podcasts on iTunes. Share a screenshot of your review on social media, tagging the show and/or host.
8	If you don't have a recent, professional image, get one taken. Remember to check Groupon.com for a J.C. Penny or other special deal. Comment on at least three blogs from your list of podcasts. Retweet or otherwise share social posts of at least five podcast hosts from shows that have passed your screening. Review one of the podcasts on iTunes. Share a screenshot of your review on social media, tagging the show and/or host.

DAY	ACTIVITY
9	Answer the questions at the end of Chapter __ to determine your expert profile. Write a fifty-word introduction as an expert you feel confident in sharing with the host, listeners, friends, and family. Comment on at least three blogs from your list of podcasts. Retweet or otherwise share social posts of at least five podcast hosts from shows that have passed your screening. Review one of the podcasts on iTunes. Share a screenshot of your review on social media, tagging the show and/or host.
10	Check your public profiles on social sites like Facebook, Twitter, LinkedIn, and Instagram. Are there any that you need to protect? Any content you should add or remove? Any that need to be deleted entirely? If you don't have a website, create a simple starter website. If you need help, go to the resources page at www.PodcastGuestProfits.com/Resources. Comment on at least three blogs from your list of podcasts. Retweet or otherwise share social posts of at least five podcast hosts from shows that have passed your screening. Review one of the podcasts on iTunes. Share a screenshot of your review on social media, tagging the show and/or host.

DAY	ACTIVITY
11	Head on over to the resources page at www.PodcastGuestProfits.com/Resources and either order one of the Podcast Equipment Bundles we have listed there or download the Podcast Equipment Checklist and purchase at least one of the quality USB microphones for you to make sure you have high-quality audio to match your high quality content. Comment on at least three blogs from your list of podcasts. Retweet or otherwise share social posts of at least five podcast hosts from shows that have passed your screening. Review one of the podcasts on iTunes. Share a screenshot of your review on social media, tagging the show and/or host.
12	Make a list of ten offers your ideal customer might value enough to exchange their contact information with you. Comment on at least three blogs from your list of podcasts. Retweet or otherwise share social posts of at least five podcast hosts from shows that have passed your screening. Review one of the podcasts on iTunes. Share a screenshot of your review on social media, tagging the show and/or host.

DAY	ACTIVITY
13	Narrow your list of ten offers down to the three you think are the highest value. Create the first iteration of those top three offers. Remember, it doesn't need to be fancy. Comment on at least three blogs from your list of podcasts. Retweet or otherwise share social posts of at least five podcast hosts from shows that have passed your screening. Review one of the podcasts on iTunes. Share a screenshot of your review on social media, tagging the show and/or host.
14	Create or have someone create your Perfect Pitch Sheet. Comment on at least three blogs from your list of podcasts. Retweet or otherwise share social posts of at least five podcast hosts from shows that have passed your screening. Review one of the podcasts on iTunes. Share a screenshot of your review on social media, tagging the show and/or host.

DAY	ACTIVITY
15	Design your first welcome page. If you need help with this go to the resources page at www.PodastGuestProfits.com/Resources. This one will be a generic template but will be duplicated and customized as you begin to land interviews. Comment on at least three blogs from your list of podcasts. Retweet or otherwise share social posts of at least five podcast hosts from shows that have passed your screening. Review one of the podcasts on iTunes. Share a screenshot of your review on social media, tagging the show and/or host.
16	Set up a calendar scheduling system like Calendly.com, Time Trade, or ScheduleOnce.com so you can prepare to pitch podcasts. If you need help with this head on over to the resources page. Ask three friends to review your pitch sheet. Make any changes you agree with. Comment on at least three blogs from your list of podcasts. Retweet or otherwise share social posts of at least five podcast hosts from shows that have passed your screening. Review one of the podcasts on iTunes. Share a screenshot of your review on social media, tagging the show and/or host.

DAY	ACTIVITY
17	Send an e-mail to at least five podcasts asking to be a guest. Choose five where you have developed the closest relationships to date. Don't worry. You're ready. Comment on at least three blogs from your list of podcasts. Retweet or otherwise share social posts of at least five podcast hosts from shows that have passed your screening. Review one of the podcasts on iTunes. Share a screenshot of your review on social media, tagging the show and/or host.
18	Send an e-mail to at least five more podcasts asking to be a guest. Choose five where you have developed the closest relationships to date. Comment on at least three blogs from your list of podcasts. Retweet or otherwise share social posts of at least five podcast hosts from shows that have passed your screening. Review one of the podcasts on iTunes. Share a screenshot of your review on social media, tagging the show and/or host.

DAY	ACTIVITY
19	By this point your activities will be directed in part by your system. As you land more interviews you will need to be making welcome pages, refining offers, updating your pitch sheet, etc. No matter what your success is to date, you need to constantly be identifying, screening, and networking with podcasts and hosts, to pitch to be a guest. By this point you may be strongly considering outsourcing as well. Thus, even if you don't want to start outsourcing yet, start to identify the items that you can outsource using the guide in Chapter __. Comment on at least three blogs from your list of podcasts. Retweet or otherwise share social posts of at least five podcast hosts from shows that have passed your screening. Review one of the podcasts on iTunes. Share a screenshot of your review on social media, tagging the show and/or host.

DAY	ACTIVITY
20	Sign up for an e-mail marketing solution like Mailchimp, Aweber, or ConvertKit. If you need help with this go the resources page. Begin building your funnel to collect contact information and deliver your offers through your welcome page. Test out your system using your personal e-mail address to make sure it's working. Comment on at least three blogs from your list of podcasts. Retweet or otherwise share social posts of at least five podcast hosts from shows that have passed your screening. Review one of the podcasts on iTunes. Share a screenshot of your review on social media, tagging the show and/or host.
21	Now that you're three weeks in, assess what you have struggled with so far. What was easier than expected? What was harder? What did you struggle with? You might find some tasks to outsource to free yourself up to concentrate on preparing for interviews and doing the tasks you enjoy and are excellent at.

DAY	ACTIVITY
22	After three weeks, your process will likely be starting to yield some interviews. Your activities will continue to be dictated by your progress and interviews. It's important to continue to pitch and network to keep your schedule full, so continue to send at least two pitches each day, review podcasts on iTunes, comment on blogs, and share and connect on social media.
23	Conduct activities needed based on progress. Consider who you could outsource to in order to shift into overdrive. It's important to continue to pitch and network to keep your schedule full, so continue to send at least two pitches each day, review podcasts on iTunes, comment on blogs, and share and connect on social media.
24	Conduct activities needed based on progress. It's important to continue to pitch and network to keep your schedule full, so continue to send at least two pitches each day, review podcasts on iTunes, comment on blogs, and share and connect on social media.

DAY	ACTIVITY
25	Conduct activities needed based on progress. It's important to continue to pitch and network to keep your schedule full, so continue to send at least two pitches each day, review podcasts on iTunes, comment on blogs, and share and connect on social media.
26	Conduct activities needed based on progress. It's important to continue to pitch and network to keep your schedule full, so continue to send at least two pitches each day, review podcasts on iTunes, comment on blogs, and share and connect on social media.
27	Conduct activities needed based on progress. It's important to continue to pitch and network to keep your schedule full, so continue to send at least two pitches each day, review podcasts on iTunes, comment on blogs, and share and connect on social media.
28	Conduct activities needed based on progress. It's important to continue to pitch and network to keep your schedule full, so continue to send at least two pitches each day, review podcasts on iTunes, comment on blogs, and share and connect on social media.

DAY	ACTIVITY
29	Conduct activities needed based on progress. It's important to continue to pitch and network to keep your schedule full, so continue to send at least two pitches each day, review podcasts on iTunes, comment on blogs, and share and connect on social media.
30	Conduct activities needed based on progress. It's important to continue to pitch and network to keep your schedule full, so continue to send at least two pitches each day, review podcasts on iTunes, comment on blogs, and share and connect on social media.